LEADERSHIP TAKES COURAGE

*How to Master Leadership - A Fable of
Transformation with Proven Techniques*

DAVID ECKER

DEDICATION

To my wife, Allison, and son, Josh, whose unwavering love and support have brightened every step of my life's journey. Without your encouragement, I could not have written these words that nurtured innovation and creativity on these pages. Through all of life's challenges, their love and our family are the heart and soul of my life.

Our journey to see the world wouldn't have been worth it without experiencing the journey with you. I am grateful for your constant presence as we embarked on our own Wolf's Path, navigating each day with an ever-present positive outlook on the next day.

I also want to thank the remarkable leaders, insightful students, alumni, and colleagues. Their stories and wisdom have illuminated the path to fostering exceptional leadership teams. Your contributions have enriched my understanding and allowed me to share valuable insights on enhancing leadership with the world. Thank you for being beacons of inspiration on this collective journey. I value your friendship each day of my life.

INTRODUCTION

Teams are a freaking mess. Most leaders can't fix teams. Everyone has had good and bad experiences. This has caused us to have a love-hate relationship with teams. I want to demonstrate how you can change teams to be more productive and work efficiently.

Colleagues blame the team when it fails, but it's not a specific team's fault. If a team fails, a leader is responsible for ensuring the team ultimately succeeds. Great leaders take on the responsibility for failure and give credit to their teams when there is a success. They don't need the limelight; their goal is to complete the project with everyone contributing toward completion.

You can be that great leader who empowers your team to go above and beyond in every aspect of work. It only takes learning the areas you need to develop and harnessing your inner drive to break down any obstacle.

The pandemic disrupted our lives, but I was lucky enough to have a stellar team. This team worked day and night to help first responders dealing with COVID-19. There was not enough Personal Protective Equipment (PPE); we all worked together to build face shields out of foam, 3D printers, and office supplies to ensure our first responders were safe. We did this by each taking a part of the problem, developing solutions, and working together to implement them.

I knew I had to document how we developed our team leadership style from that time. This book illustrates our thoughts, practices, and understanding of how leaders can develop themselves. When we learn from others experiences we can empower the team in a way that leads to high morale. It may seem impossible, but any team can be transformed into a group if they pride themselves on being a part of the whole.

Leadership is a skill. Only the people who have the courage to learn that skill will exceed all expectations. It's up to you to take the next steps. Do you have the courage to lead?

————

This book is broken down into three parts.

Part I: A fable to illustrate how our characters went from inexperienced leaders to learning how to guide in a way that encourages a new mindset.

Part II: A summary of each lesson.

Part III: Team-building exercises to make an effective team.

PART ONE
FABLE

Katie came running into the house, "Joe, we have a problem again! The squirrel's house is collapsing. The right-hand wall is falling into the structure. This is the second time this week. The otters have been saying the mud has been dripping from a log into their house."

Joe was beside himself, slumped in the nearest chair with his hands flopping in his lap.

Joe asked rhetorically, "Why is this happening?" After a long breath, he asked Katie, "Are we fixing the wall?"

"Yes, the team is working on the wall, but walls collapsing on new houses can't occur! Luckily, this is an easy fix, but we can't have customers perceive us like this. If word got out, we would have no new customers, meaning no business! Did you hear me. No business!" She was yelling and frustrated.

Joe put his hands up, "I know! I know! I am not sure why I am letting this happen?" He began to sob into his hands.

Katie hugged her brother.

She whispered, "I am sorry, it's not your fault; we must have missed something."

"It's my fault, I am in charge, I take full responsibility."

Summer walked into the room, "No, Joe, it's all our fault. The three of us are in charge together. We have to figure out how to fix this."

Joe knew Summer and Katie were right. It would take all three of them working together to fix whatever was happening.

At that moment, there was a banging on the door. Summer opened it to see Crane, one of their workers, standing there.

"Can I come in and talk to you?"

"Sure," Summer wondered why Crane would want to see them?

Crane stomped in. She saw Joe and Kate sitting beside each other in the adjoining room.

Crane didn't wait for Summer to catch up; she approached Joe and Katie.

In a tone that shook them both to their core, "I QUIT!" Crane continued, practically yelling, "This wall collapsing is the last straw. You are blaming me for that incident, and I won't have it. I am just the tallest and was put on the top of the roof."

Joe calmer, "What are you talking about?"

"The wall is collapsing; everyone is blaming me. I am not going to take this. If you think you are so good, you can put on top of that roof yourself." Crane said

Crane turned toward the door to leave. Summer was in utter shock; what had happened that caused this?

Joe got up and walked behind Crane.

"I am not blaming you. This wasn't your fault. It was mine." Joe said

Crane speaking under her breath, "Sure it was. You don't know what's going on. Everyone is looking for someone to blame."

"Please realize it's not me, we value you."

"Well, you don't show it. I am done!" Crane walked out the front door, slamming it without letting Joe get another word in.

They were all in shock; how could Crane, the tallest worker, just quit? What had happened that made Crane so upset?

They all sat down and did nothing for a few minutes, alone in their own thoughts. From the other room came a ding; Summer got up and went toward the sound.

"Dinner's ready!"

The three sat at the dinner table picking at their food. Joe was the first to speak as he turned to Summer.

"I am getting frustrated. I don't want others to feel the same way as Crane. I want to allow our employees more autonomy and direct less, but I am worried that more issues will occur."

"I know what you mean. The other day, we had some structural issues and time delays. I didn't tell you, but the squirrel family was upset since it took an extra two weeks to complete their house." Summer said

Kate sighed, "It wasn't our fault. We had an issue getting the right supplies. We needed a specific log to finish the roof correctly, but I wasn't able to find it. "

"Katie, it's not your fault. It's all of ours. We are missing something. We need to find a better way to organize ourselves so that whatever happens with our teams can get fixed." Joe said

Joe thought about the journey that got them together. It seems so long ago when Joe was thrown out of his mother's pack. He learned that he had to figure things out independently until Katie left the pack to be with her brother. It was good when they were together; then they met Summer, a lonely wolf who was lost. Summer had a similar experience and bonded with them immediately. They found out that to survive, they had to ask for help from others. When other animals helped them, they were able to learn the lessons that guided them to follow their passion.

"We all need to learn more about how to improve our team leadership. We all should talk to others with more experience to find out how their teams work together so we can improve our teams before something worse than Crane quitting happens." Joe said

"What is worse than that? She is the tallest animal we have on the team." Katie asked

As if Summer could read Joe's mind, she spoke up, "Before someone gets hurt."

Unspoken, all three agreed that they needed to do something.

ELEPHANTS

"Memory is helpful when you look at things over a long time."

Joe decided to sit on a rock looking out over a large lake. He gazed over the lake, trying to figure out how management would work in his new home-building organization. He knew he needed advice but didn't know where to turn. He was looking at the other animals that were near the lake, trying to figure out which would be able to give him the best advice.

Joe knew there were good and bad ways to lead teams of people. He knew he would struggle with this no matter which kind of manager he could become. But he also knew that if he didn't hear or learn about management, no matter what path he chose, he would be unable to help his people develop.

Joe was sitting there when suddenly a voice from above said, "Hi Joe."

The voice surprised Joe because he had been daydreaming. This was a quality unlike him; Joe was always alert, and this could have been a bear that could have killed him.

Joe looked up to see a giant elephant standing there. Most

wolves would be scared out of their mind when a humongous elephant looked over at them. But not Joe and not this elephant.

Joe turned and said, "Hi, Fred." Fred was a friend. Joe met him one day on the savannah. Fred was with his group that day. The wolf and elephant each looked like they wanted to attack, but something sparked them to talk to each other instead. They learned much about how each other saw the world and trusted each other from that day forward. Joe had some issues in the past, and whenever he found Fred, he was very supportive of everything Joe did.

"What's wrong? Joe, you look like you're troubled?"

"No, just thinking about management and how to implement it."

Fred laughed. "Management? That's my area of expertise. I've been looking into it and talking to people about management for years. We elephants have long memories, so we know all about leadership and how to lead animals. What do you want to know?"

"Do you know about team management? Can you share some information on how to be effective?"

"Of course, Joe. Would you mind walking to the watering hole as we talk?"

"Sure."

Fred said as they walked toward the watering hole, "The first thing you must know about team management is that it's an art form. Leading is helping people in a precise way so they can complete the objectives. It's a simple idea, but everyone makes it very complex. If you want animals to achieve the group goal, you must help them achieve their personal goals."

Joe looked puzzled by this statement. "What did you mean by group goals versus their personal goals?"

"Teams try to make projects complex by gathering lots of

various little problems and grouping them together so that they can be solved. Thinking that all these details are part of the bigger objective. Instead of realizing, when they have all these issues the team loses focus on the objective. It's working on focusing them on group goals. Does that make sense?"

Joe replied, "Yes, that's exactly what I'm trying to figure out. How to ensure everyone meets our company's objectives. Any advice you could give would help me ensure I keep them on the right path to meet those objectives."

"I understand where you are coming from. We will focus on team management but remember that giving people an individual objective will help. I can cover more details on this at another time," Fred continued, "team management is moving a group of animals toward solving a complex issue."

"Correct, it's getting the team to work together to solve an issue or complete a project," Joe said.

"Right, let's discuss how to achieve this." Fred continued, "Team management is to ensure you communicate clear objectives. When a team understands what is expected, they are able to create a plan toward that objective. Your role is to clarify the objective, describe the details, then let them ask questions. The ability to answer all questions will allow each team member to understand the goal."

"I get it. Communicate and answer questions" Joe replied.

"For example, if we needed to find a new place to graze. Our group leader would ensure that all our younger elephants have grazed and have gotten enough water before we move on. The leader would make sure the objectives are clear. We need to find a new spot to graze, we are all prepared for a long walk and watch over each other so no one is left behind until we reach the destination. Our team leader understands all this and communicates these critical components for the journey," Fred asked, "does this mean the group leader is a good or bad manager?"

"Good."

"You're right, he listed the objective and the success criteria needed to meet the objective. When teams are working together, they need both. When you are running your company, do you set both?" Fred said

Joe admitted, "No, I only focus on the objective."

"That is good, but without a documented success criterion, how do you know your team completes all the steps in the project?" Fred asked.

"We don't! This is an area we lack. We have been going by what they tell us, not what is written down. We have many satisfied customers, but others were not thrilled because we missed a couple of their needs."

"That happens. You can fix it by writing down success criteria like a checklist then when everything is checked off the project has met objectives." Fred said

"Great, I got this!"

"Joe please realize that bad team management can creep in very quickly. We need to prevent your team leaders from micromanaging the teams. You must be empowering them to grow."

Joe said, "That's confusing,"

"Yep. Team management isn't easy, and people think it's this simple idea, but it is rather tricky if done well. One of the key times things get difficult is when you have simultaneous objectives. Team managers sometimes get stressed and lose focus, putting undue pressure on the team by wanting to know every task and setting deadlines to complete it. "

Having reached the watering hole, Fred took a drink of water.

Fred continued, "The term micromanager is someone we see as a kind of manager who doesn't allow his people to do anything without permission. They do this because they feel they need more control over the situation than anyone else in their company. This makes sense sometimes because managers want to ensure they can provide customers with the best possible product or service. But it affects morale within the company."

"How do you tell if this is starting within the company?" Joe asked.

"Managers who micromanage their employees ask for numerous updates daily on what is going on with the projects. Sometimes, even managers in high-level positions want hourly updates. When a team leader is only writing updates or attending useless meetings, they are inefficient and have low morale. This low morale ends up being like a virus and infecting the team. The team spends most of their time writing reports without ever getting anything done toward project goals," Fred replied.

"Micromanaging is bad. Leaders who do this lack the focus to meet the objectives of the team and are unable to help them grow. I will be aware of it in my organization. Thank you."

Fred stopped and looked at Joe a second and said directly. "This is going to happen to you!"

Joe looked stunned. *How could Fred know this would happen to me? It won't*, he thought. He would allow others to do what they needed.

"It happens to every new team manager, but if you're able to recognize when it's going on, you'll be more prepared to get out of the situation quickly. Once you identify it, focus on what you're trying to achieve with the team versus that specific situation that you feel needs to be micromanaged."

Joe asked, "What are the signs of a micromanager so that I can recognize them and avoid them?"

"It's hard to say precisely why people go down this road. But from memory, what I've seen is when they have their insecurities about something going on in their life that affects their ability to see a larger picture in a company or organization. The only way they are able to feel better is to have complete control of the situation."

Joe and Fred paused. It was like Fred was searching his mind for the right example to share.

"One situation that comes to mind, a team was working on upgrading a new water supply to a lake. The team manager pulled them off to work on flooding, which ended up dominating their time. Their supervisors wanted reports, meeting updates, and to work non-stop to clear the flooded plains, which took months. It wasn't long before the highest levels of the company, the executives, found out. They got upset at the team leader since they never finished the new water supply for the lake. Instead of taking responsibility for the team's lack of progress, he blamed the team. He arranged for all his team members to meet with the higher-ups to explain themselves. This micromanager leader covered himself with all the reports and meeting updates but blamed the team for his failings. In an organization that has a micro-managing leader the morale is low, and team members are put in difficult situations."

Joe was in shock, and he never wanted to be a leader who micro-managed his teams and didn't think this was happening within his organization. "Is there any model you can recall that would help us to avoid this micromanaging culture and ensure we help our teams?"

"I found these ideas most effective and to apply to almost all leaders regardless of the field."

Fred continued, "First, the leader should Plow the Field to ensure the objective of growing can be completed successfully. This ensures that all the rocks, grass, and logs are removed from the field. Then, the field is turned over, and the old soil is integrated into the new soil below for planting the ground.

Allowing this new mixed soil to combine into a rich base prepares the farmer to have a fruitful crop that season."

Second, the leader needs to Catch all the Rain. When planting in a field, you need rain to grow crops. The farmer will lay out irrigation for the crops. He will ensure that the crops receive enough rain to grow. If there is a large downpour for days, it can cause flooding, bringing too much rain. Too much would wash away crops, and that season's crop will be lost. The farmer must catch the extra rain and divert it to the stream or other field. This will allow his crops to grow, and he can stay on course. The farmer is always on the watch for too much rain and the ramifications it can cause."

Third, the farmer has to be a Sounding board for the workers. The workers on the farm always have problems. A row of crops isn't getting enough sun, another area needs more fertilizer, and sometimes they fix a problem that isn't a real problem. If they let nature do its job, the problem would resolve itself. The farmer is their sounding board, allowing them to come to talk to him without judgment. He asks questions and allows his team to get to develop conclusions. By asking the farmer the right questions, the workers understand the direction they need to follow to ensure the crops grow. This interaction allows the farmer the ability to mentor and empower workers to fix problems."

Joe didn't have anything to say. Sometimes, Joe was amazed at how much his friend Fred knew. Joe was shocked because the blazing sun from above would typically make him sweat immensely, but today, he felt as relaxed as the breeze. Joe had never heard these ideas before but realized he liked what he heard. Joe refocused himself when he replied, "Those are the only three steps you need to lead a team?"

"Yep, just follow those, and you will do great!"

Fred turned, giving his friend a gentle nudge with a smile before walking off.

The ground shook as Fred walked sending vibrations through the landscape, as he got further away vibrations diminished. The vibrations calmed Joe; he knew he could trust Fred's advice and accomplish these three steps.

ZEBRAS

Joe knew from Fred's lesson he had to let Summer and Katie grow into their roles and let them learn lessons, both good and bad. Joe had to teach them to have the same discussions he had with animals to develop their own path.

Joe explained to Summer, "Teams are necessary for any leader to move any idea forward. We have heard that entrepreneurs are passionate about moving any idea forward, sometimes willing it to exist. Our view has always been hard work gives us a passion for success. It's time that you help the leadership team by talking to other animals."

Summer was hesitant, "Joe, why me? You have been doing a great job."

"Summer, you can do this. It is new to you, but you have seen how it helped us to find purpose. I know this will help you to develop."

Summer was not thrilled; when she had gone out to do things with her pack earlier in life by herself, the result wasn't positive. When she failed, the pack confronted her. They verbally put her down and told her she was a failure when they should have been supportive. These feelings from that time started to bubble up inside of her, and tears began forming in her eyes.

Joe sensed her trepidation and said, "Summer, I and Katie are going to go with you. I will stay slightly behind so you can do all the talking."

Summer felt relieved. Initially, she thought she was being sent out alone, which was one of her biggest fears. Joe was not doing this; his objective was for her to grow by finding out information that could help them do better. She knew this was one way he was supporting her.

"OK, Let's go!" She was not ready to do this, but she knew she wouldn't do this without the push from Joe.

Summer, Joe, and Katie ventured out.

Summer said, "I will take the lead." Joe and Katie nodded in agreement.

Summer took the lead. She had met Joe and Katie almost two years ago when she was out on her own; trying to survive in this nasty world. Each of them had experienced disappointment and grief, and her pack continued to put her down when she was growing up. They made her an outcast among her family. Summer was depressed, lost in the world, but didn't know it. She was able to escape her family pack to live on her own. She was always on edge that her family would come back to ridicule and blame her for their shortcomings. When she stumbled on her two new friends who had just had similar experiences to hers, it made Summer not feel so alone. It changed her worldview and excited her about doing things in the world again. She had found a new, renewed purpose through discussions with Joe. His words gave her a positive mindset where she knew she could accomplish anything.

Summer had taken on the responsibility of building a new team for their business. Summer didn't know how to assemble a team, and neither did Joe or Katie. They had been winging it, which she knew wasn't the best way to proceed.

Joe said to her. "I have complete confidence that you will bring together the right group to help us."

Those words helped her be inspired that someone trusted her. Joe was the type of wolf who was there for her when needed.

Summer knew of only one other team that seemed to work in perfect unison. That was the zebras she had met some time ago. Summer was nervous about approaching them alone since they had a herd of at least fifty that could easily trample her.

The zebras were nomadic, so they weren't always in the area you would expect. Summer knew they spent time in the open grasslands that seemed to go to the horizon. Luckily, she started her search at one of the watering holes outside the forest. They weren't there, but she discovered them by the lake, grazing and drinking.

Summer approached slowly; almost immediately, the zebras shifted around positions in the herd. The smaller zebras were moved to the inside of the circle while others positioned themselves outside. There were always a few zebras standing next to each other just on the outside of the ring, but one would face one way, and the other would face the opposite way. This was their way of being on guard for predators. A wolf like her was a threat to them. The two opposing zebras could see everything that happened from either direction and quickly notified the herd.

Summer said, "Excuse me, but can anyone tell me how you formed your herd?"

The zebras pretended not to hear her. They made some

noises, and hoofs started to push around. The dirt under their legs splashed up into the air. It didn't seem like they heard Summer, but she was determined to forge ahead.

"My apologies for bothering you, but," Summer tried to say.

The Zebra on the left side of a row within the circle said, "You aren't bothering us as long as we aren't going to get eaten. We can share the watering hole with you."

"Thank you, but I need to learn about teams. I have watched you as a herd, and you care deeply about each other. Why do you do that?"

"One second," The Zebra replied. There were a ton of noises and groans from the group of zebras. It seemed to Summer this was a way of communicating in a language she didn't understand.

A few zebras started to shuffle positions, and then it seemed the whole herd changed. It was like a big dance moving in a circle as they moved backward and forward, some in a circle, others in a straight path. This was all strange to her.

As they moved, one of the zebras stood in front. Other zebras stood near them, facing forward and some facing back to Summer. The movement was continuing around and behind them. Other zebras stood all around as if they were all on guard, keeping her safe.

Looking at her, Zebra said, "Why do you want to know about our herd? Are you trying to learn how to hunt us?"

"No, I am working with my friends." Summer gestured to her friends Joe and Katie, sitting calmly a few yards away in the grass.

The zebras noticed them, but they were in the low grass, not trying to hide themselves. They didn't look like the usual attack positions they had seen from other predators.

Summer continued, "We own a business building houses,

but we are having trouble building a team. We are hoping that you could give us some advice on how to put a team together. I have watched how your group walks together, helps, and cares about each other. I thought you would be a good group to learn from."

The Zebra was in utter shock. Why would this wolf talk to them about teams? They knew how to work together and protect each other, but that is just something the zebras have always done. It then dawned on the lead zebra that this was something that he hadn't seen other animals do in their travels. He was one of the oldest zebras and kept up their traditions but wasn't always paying attention to other animals. His focus has always been inward toward the herd.

The Zebra said, "Sure, we can offer some guidance to you about your task. Let me explain a little about our herd. We are made up of young ones less than a year old, middle-aged, our most robust, and then older zebras like myself that have a long knowledge. The older zebras are the ones that teach the traditions that guide us."

"Traditions are our stories that we use in our herd to explain how and why we do things in a particular way. Let me tell you the lone zebra story."

"The Lone Zebra, where one of our friends decided it was best to venture alone to explore the world. This zebra was focused on independence and drive. They felt they could explore the world to learn how others survived in this landscape. We suggested that we put a team together to go with him, but he was determined to do this on his own. He was a stubborn and proud zebra. At the time, I didn't realize that he was hurting inside and could have used more support, but we let him go out alone. He was gone no more than four days when he came running back to the herd with at least two packs of lions on his tail. The lions saw us and were more

excited to hunt the whole herd. When we are in a herd of zebras, they look to find easy prey. The zebra who left ran straight into the middle of the herd. This immediately put us out of form since some of his friends were in the center of the herd. He hoped they would quickly accept him back into the herd and protect him. His foolishness changed our protection circle, exposing some of the young zebras. Luckily, we moved our circle to a different formation since we saw the lions. Even with that, we weren't quick enough, and we lost ten zebras that day. All because this lone zebra didn't follow our traditions. "

The Zebra finished, "This is a story told to each of our newborns. This is why we stay together and always have zebras facing the opposite way. They are on guard duty looking out to protect the herd."

"Traditions are something I never considered. Stories like the one you told illustrate how it is not about the individual member. It's about the herd. Things would run smoothly if you could get everyone in the herd to understand this. Is that what you mean?" Summer replied

"Yes and no. Yes, we could get the zebra herd together, but any member of our herd is still an individual. Individual zebras are all different from our strips to our personalities. There is nothing wrong with differences. We need to continue to embrace each other for shared success."

"Are these stories your key to teaching each other?" Summer asked.

"Yes, we use stories to illustrate points. These allow each herd member to remember that their actions impact others," The Zebra replied.

Summer didn't quite get it but understood that teams are made up of individuals. Each of them has their own thoughts, but by following the stories, they follow a path that has helped them survive in the wilderness. She was confused but knew she would have to reflect on this.

"Are there other things the herd does that make it so efficient?" Summer asked

"We follow certain guiding principles that we agree on when we are born. These guiding principles are that the elders are wise and are always respected. The second is that leaders may not always explain everything immediately when something occurs, but ask questions, be patient, and work toward a common goal."

"Wait did you just say you have two guiding principles?" Summer was surprised.

"Yes, let me briefly break this down for you. The first one is the elders are wise and should be respected. This comes from our point of view: if you can live for such a long time, you are doing things right. We need to learn the elders' experiences, so we live good lives. It can be challenging since sometimes they are slower than others. They can teach us things we have forgotten or never had time to learn if we respect them. Zebras cannot write down information, so we use the elder's knowledge to give us the ability to share information from one generation to the next. Remind me before you leave to introduce you to our eldest member of the herd. They can teach you about knowledge."

"Ok, I will try to remember," Summer's memory was always bad, she was sure she would forget.

The Zebra stopped for a second, then continued, "We always need to consider how we complete a task; when we don't have a process, we create one. The elders can give us feedback to ensure we don't waste time doing something that has already been tried many times. We don't mind experimentation but ensure it's not wasted on things put in place for everyone's benefit."

The Zebra coughed, "Can we walk back toward the lake? All this talking is making me dry." Summer nodded, and they began to walk. Almost immediately, a noise came out of the zebra's mouth. It was a dull hoot-type noise, but it was enough that the herd understood. Two zebras got in front of the elder zebra, and a line formed behind them. Summer looked behind them as they walked, and the line seemed to go on for miles. She wondered what they were doing.

Summer decided she needed to ask what had happened. "Why are they lining up, one behind each other?"

"For the safety of each individual, the predators get confused by us lining up. They don't see us as a big herd. They see single individual members in this formation. The predator (for example, a Lion) would only go after one of the zebras in line. They miss the rest of the herd that is in line. When an attack occurs, we can warn others in the herd in front or behind that an attack is happening. They can flee or protect the herd." The Zebra shared.

"Smart!" She looked ahead at the watering home only a few steps away.

The lead zebras made it to the watering hole first. They checked the surroundings and acknowledged the area was clear. The elder zebra was not as worried as usual since he had a wolf beside him. Usually, he would be running in the other direction if that occurred, but with a wolf standing there, it was a good deterrent from any other predator trying to attack them.

After they got their drink, the elder zebra walked up the hill so the line could continue to get water. The Zebra said, "Oh, where was I in the story?"

Summer replied, "I think you were going to tell me about leaders not explaining things immediately and patience."

"Oh Yes! You are correct. Thank you so much for remembering my place. As I get older, there are memory lapses. We want to be young and fast forever, but that's not reality."

"I understand, but you look great."

The Zebra had a large grin and pushed Summer ever so lightly. "Leaders are not born into that role in our herd. It takes hard work to earn a role. The herd then votes for who they feel has developed to become a leader. This process allows leaders to grow within the herd. The line leader is an example. She works at mentoring younger zebras before being offered that position. The mentorship helped other zebras develop. She demonstrates to younger members the ability to keep the herd safe and understand where our favorite places are located. This demonstrated to the herd that she could be trusted, so they offered her the line leader role. Her role is to keep the line organized and ensure our safety and security when near any body of water. Did you know that a year or so ago, we were at a watering hole a long way from here? Near the plateau of the setting sun. Our line leader was checking the perimeter of a watering hole, but an impatient zebra didn't want to wait. He was running toward the watering hole when a Hippopotamus jumped out. The Hippo would have bitten the young zebra if the line leader hadn't been ready. She stood up to the Hippo, and several other zebras made noise, so the Hippo went back into the water away from the herd. It was her quick thinking that saved the young zebra's life."

"Wow, that is impressive. That's an important role for that leader."

"It is essential; we want a line leader to have good eyesight and hearing. They would not be of any value in this role if they didn't." The Zebra said

"So, you have requirements for different leaders?"

"Yes, we only want new leaders that want to do the job. You must always ensure you have the right leaders in the right places. Sometimes, a leader is selected but isn't put in the right role. We figure out as quickly as possible that this fit isn't correct. We then work to find them a better role."

Summer replied. "That's a good point. Some animals have specific skills, like beavers who have teeth that can get through any wood, while others can think critically about issues and provide solutions. I understand that since Katie, Joe, and I have different expertise to offer our business. I am sure it's the same in your herd."

"Yes, it is. We all have skills that help us live, and we work to embrace everyone's expertise. For example, we could have a zebra that talks a lot, but if they don't have any knowledge to impart, the talking is just useless banter. When we seek leaders, we want ones that can be solid as a rock. We look for driven, dedicated leaders, good communicators, and listeners. They will be a perfect choice if you can find a leader with these four qualities."

"Do you often find leaders with all these qualities?"

Zebra laughed for a minute before replying. "No, that is our ideal. We find leaders with two or three qualities then we work to develop the rest within our community."

"The elders know that a good leader is not perfect, but you must ask yourself. Will this leader be able to communicate effectively? We ask our fellow leaders, will this new zebra be someone who would help push them to their solution or assist others to develop? Are they able to learn from their mistakes and admit when they happen? Good leaders embrace all these qualities to ensure the herd doesn't suffer. Overall, we need a leader that thinks about the herd vs the individual."

The Zebra thought for a long, hard minute. As if wrestling with the right words. The Zebra was taking his time deliberately. He wanted to make sure he said it correctly so Summer could understand what leading a team was in their minds.

After waiting a while, Summer replied, "You ok?"

"Yes, I was trying to impart some information but wanted to get the right phrase together. Leaders are not the key to keeping the herd together. Our goal is efficiency for the herd, and leaders are our guide toward that goal."

Summer was surprised, "Did you just say your leaders are not the key? Then who is?" Summer was defeated; she spent all this time and hadn't gotten anywhere. She would disappoint Joe and Katie, the two people in the world she would never want to disappoint.

"Everyone is the key. Our leaders may set our path, but the herd works together to get us to our objectives. Each herd member is given a role to contribute to the herd. Such as watching out for the elderly members, teaching the younger ones, security, safety, mentorship, or education. Whatever role they have been given is important for the herd to meet its goal. When you look at your team, what keeps you together working efficiently?"

Summer was taken aback a little. She hadn't expected that question but thought it was a fair question to ask.

"Trust is an integral part of our leadership team; it's something that we have developed over time."

"Exactly. That is how you ensure your team works together."

Summer couldn't have agreed more; she knew this team was special. Her speaking to a Zebra a year ago would have been unheard of before she met Joe and Katie. Summer was learning how to survive on her own. Why would she care about anything else, but that is different now. She realized she could be part of something bigger that would give her a sense of pride. She could feel this pride, which resonated from her pores, whiskers, and head. Listening to the Zebra, she was beginning to understand the value of a trusting team. It would be the same for building the new team in the company.

Summer asked, "I want to ensure I understand. Leadership is about helping and guiding, but the herd works together to meet the goal. Your overarching goal is efficiency."

"Exactly."

Summer understood that leadership in their herd had a mutual relationship with everyone on the team. It wasn't what she expected, but she knew this would help her as they formed their group.

"There is one more thing I need to share to help you build your herd. It is talking. It's the lifeblood of our herd."

Summer was confused again. She was getting this, and then Zebra threw her a curveball.

"Lifeblood? Isn't talking something you normally do?" Summer asked

"We do a lot of talking, but it is intentional in our case. We talk about the weather, the taste of the grass, the level of the watering hole, why two of our herd are fighting over a female, how the younger ones are walking, and even why the sun is going down. We don't know all the answers to these questions, but we spend more time talking than eating. Which you can imagine can cause some chaos in the herd."

The Zebra took a breath then continued

"I often wonder how we get anything done with all the talking that we do. I may joke about it, but it is the best thing any herd can do to be successful."

"Why is talking so key? Everyone does it. It's a way of sharing information." Summer asked

"Yes, it is easy, but since we have no secrets in our herd, the talking helps keep it out in the open. As soon as you say something to a zebra in the community, everyone tells everyone else within a short period. It is excellent for morale and transparency, which are essential when you want to get anything done."

Summer asked thoughtfully, "Why do you think constant communication is important for the herd?"

"The communication allows everyone to feel connected. Being more connected allows the older elders to be more relaxed. They don't feel that anyone would put them out to pasture. It allows us to know what each other thinks and not have motives outside the group's interests. Which in turn, allows everyone to be part of the herd."

"This is the transparency I heard about in organizations. Does it work?" Summer Asked.

"Transparency works most times; zebras then know about decisions that different leaders make. We all know the goal, and the decisions are focused on how to meet that objective. Sometimes decisions cause some tension in the herd, but when this happens, a leader will address it individually. If the individual zebra is still upset, the leaders will work together to hear this zebra out. They will always find some way of understanding all the reasonable requests and finding a way to offer a solution. This resolves the issue, and it works out well. We always know that no individual zebra is doing anything to harm others. Usually, their objection is from a point of view that may not have been considered. Once it is shared it will be considered for all future decisions."

Summer was nodding along with The Zebra as he talked.

"I know I have spoken more today than I have in a while. Did you find this helpful?"

Summer had a big smile as if someone had just given her a beautiful gift that she didn't expect, "Yes, that is perfect. You shared great details on how to make team leadership work. I have a lot to do, but your information set me on my path. Thank you so much."

"You are welcome." The Zebra said. Summer turned to leave and began to walk where Joe and Katie were sitting.

"One more thing, talking will always help any situation. If you have any more questions, please come by and ask. I enjoyed talking to you."

"Thank you, I enjoyed talking to you too."

Summer reached where Joe and Katie sat and plopped down on the ground. She was so exhausted as if she had just run twenty miles to catch a deer. Summer was physically exhausted from the long talk with the zebra. Summer had never had such a great and exhausting experience at the same time, but she knew that sharing it with Joe and Katie would help.

"Yes, it's just exhausting talking so much but I learned a lot. Give me a minute to explain". Joe and Katie waited to listen when Summer was ready.

Summer took a few minutes to organize her thoughts, Joe and Katie were patiently waiting. Joe knew this was all new for Summer, but she needed to get out of her comfort zone. This is one of those things he wanted her to experience. If she was able to gain this knowledge and share it with them, then they all knew it could be implemented. This opportunity for Summer to talk to the Zebra was her place where she could grow and develop.

Summer started explaining what she learned, "The first lesson I learned is about traditions, also known as stories) that need to be shared with each member of the team. We may have a tradition that we didn't even realize. Do you remember that we built a house for the raccoon family first because they offered part of their house not only as a shelter for them but also to be used by others while those wait for their home. This is a tradition we have followed since we started the business. Right?"

Joe and Katie nodded their heads in the affirmative. This story from when they started is still happening today; the raccoons are hosting some possums in their house now. While the possums are waiting for their new house to be finished.

"This is our tradition, that we have been doing since our inception. This is a tradition that we need to teach any new members of the team. Regardless of the role in the team, our traditions must be shared. These traditions that we communicate demonstrate what we feel is important for the team and that we feel is vital for our success. If the new team member hasn't learned our traditions, how would we ever expect them to meet objectives in the way we have planned them."

Joe thought about this for a minute, and he wanted to make sure he understood what she had learned.

"You are saying that we need to share our stories with everyone on the team to ensure they understand the values in our business."

"EXACTLY! By doing this, we will ensure that each person on the team has heard our stories; these are the reasons that demonstrate why we are in this business. It's these stories that pave the way for them to do their jobs effectively." Summer said.

"That makes sense; I would never have thought about that."

"The second lesson is the zebras have developed a mutual respect for the oldest members of their herd. They are taught that these members are the holders of their history and should always have high respect. They feel that these elders hold their wisdom and understanding, which sets them apart from other animals. As the zebra spoke, I was thinking of the Hyena who seemed always to be chasing the same bird or animal. They don't seem to be learning from their past experiences. The zebras have a collection of knowledge that is shared with the herd. This allows them to try new ways of doing things. This makes them more efficient and faster at completing tasks."

Joe said, "Always respect them; that's a good point." Joe had never really thought deeply about his elders. From his experience in the past, the wolf pack was made of independent wolves just following a leader blindly. They had never actually respected anyone, but having a pack that respected each other, especially the older ones, is appealing.

"Would that mean I would have to listen and do what the elderly say all the time?" Katie asked Summer.

"I don't think you have to do what they say, but you should listen to the knowledge they share. I didn't get the impression that each of them followed the elder's way of doing things, but I got that they listened and felt the knowledge they gain through interactions is valuable."

"That would be doable. I am a young wolf, but I could gain a lot from someone with more experience than me." Katie replied.

"I think that is the objective. If you learn from the ways of the past, you can help shape the future."

Joe was still sitting quietly listening and agreed with Katie. Learning from the elders is vitally important in any team. When he was young, Joe had heard that packs of wolves put the older members on the outside so they could be prey. They were treated as just hangers-on, not members of the pack anymore. This always bothered Joe; why couldn't they participate and share their knowledge? He heard from his friends that when these elderly members of the pack speak, the young members of the leadership group would dismiss them or not even acknowledge they were speaking. This would be different in the team he wanted to lead. The Zebra was right; we need to respect and value the elders. This might be a new concept, but this value offers many benefits.

Joe had no idea how to implement this. He would have to work with Summer and Katie to develop a strategy that would showcase and respect the elderly team members throughout the organization.

Joe was scared about how long this would take to implement but didn't want to reveal this to Summer or Katie. His vulnerability came from a wanting to make change quickly based on what Summer had learned, but he wasn't sure he was up for the task even though Fred had confidence in him. He had to wrap his mind around that things change over time.

"The last lesson I learned was—" Summer said,

All of a sudden, Katie jumped on Joe. Joe was lying on the ground with his sister on top of him; he pushed her off, ran up to her, and pounced on his sister. She wasn't this tiny wolf anymore; she was big and hard to push down. They wrestled for a few moments in the grass.

"Why did you do that?" Joe asked.

"You needed it; you had this all-serious face. That the world was closing in on you. You need to remember we are all in this together. OK?" Katie replied.

Joe was more relaxed now and said, "Yes, I am, thank you."

He turned to Summer, who was smiling and wanted to join in the fun but knew brother and sister needed the time. Joe walked over to Summer and pushed her with his shoulders.

Summer pushed back with a bigger smile and said, "You want to play old man. I can push you down pretty hard."

"I know you can. I am not looking to pick a fight." He had a big smile on his face. He loved Summer, and she knew that.

"I know. As I was saying, the last lesson I learned was simple. Talk about what is going on; don't have any secrets. Share what's on your mind, both the positive and negative without being confrontational. Suppose we can do this and listen to what is being said without reacting. We can ensure that everyone is on the same page. I also learned that zebras talk a lot. They seem to talk more than they do anything else. It was funny!"

"We can do that; we seem to communicate all the time," Katie commented.

"It's constant communication that makes people feel

comfortable about changes in the organization. It's when the changes occur without the ability to ask questions and get honest answers when the teams start to falter. This causes mistakes in the whole organization." Summer replied.

"We don't want that. We will need to ensure communication is across the organization."

Katie, Joe, and Summer stood there and smiled at each other as they began to walk.

MEERKATS

The sun woke up. Katie was the first to see the sunrise coming over the vast land. Katie always felt that the sun brought a new uplifting feeling toward the day. No matter what occurred each day, the sun brought the prospect of adventure, excitement, and joy. Summer got up a few minutes later, looked around, and ran off into the woods. She has a routine: every morning, she scouts out what's all around to ensure they are safe. It's a practice she started many years ago when she was young and alone.

Joe was slowly waking up. Yesterday was a long day, and the extra few minutes of sitting down to understand everything that Summer learned was good for him to process. As Joe sat there, he was trying to figure out the next step on their journey to develop their business.

Katie looked out over the land, seeing many animals in the wilderness. Living their lives each day in peace and prosperity. Katie was amazed at how everything functioned seamlessly. She was always so curious about the world.

Joe turned to Katie, "Good morning. How are you doing this morning? "

"Excellent, it's a beautiful day, and the world is in our hands. I feel I can tackle any of our problems today." Katie replied.

"I know what you mean; it is empowering. We have to figure out our next steps. I think when Summer returns, we head north. We will find something we are looking for in that direction."

"Really? Why do you think north?"

"I am not sure, but it's a feeling that if we go that way, we will find the next step." Joe said.

"I feel that it will be an exciting day, so let's go that way." Katie pointed her head in the direction that Joe had indicated.

Summer soon returned, "Good morning."

Both Katie and Joe replied at the same time, "Good morning. How was your scouting session?"

"Great. There is a path leading north, which I think would be the best way to proceed." Summer motioned in the same direction Katie and Joe had just mentioned. Joe had no idea about the path or how Summer chose the direction, but it was funny that they chose the same direction. It must have been faith that pointed them all in the same way.

They followed Summer; the path was a narrow, dirt path that had leaves along both sides. The foliage along the sides blended in different parts of the path; you could see how it was well-traveled, but it could easily be lost if you weren't paying attention. Joe was amazed by the tracks of elephants, rhinos, and cheetahs. How could they walk through the brush and be aware of their surroundings? He would never know. He kept looking for a way to get through all the brush, but when he thought he had a way, it would disappear as quickly as it appeared. It seemed like he was lost in the underbrush, but he knew he wasn't completely lost because he could always just follow the tracks. The dense land gave them the cover that helped them avoid bears, a wolf's worst fear.

As they emerged, they were out in the safari landscape. Ahead, they could see a group of Meerkats working together in the field.

Katie was determined to see if these Meerkats could talk to her. She had seen them all working together; she hoped they could provide her with guidance.

Katie learned from Joe talking to the other animals that they had learned so much. It was her turn to go outside of her comfort zone. Katie walked up to the Meerkats that were going from burrow to burrow. She didn't think they noticed her. Joe and Summer were slightly behind her. Joe thought these Meerkats were quick and kept to themselves. Why would they speak to us? He was so proud that Katie was growing up and having the courage to take the initiative to talk with other animals about leadership.

Katie got closer, and then all of a sudden, the Meerkats scattered in a dozen different directions, running to hide from the wolf that they thought was there to chase and eat them. Normally, they would be correct; the pack of wolves would chase and catch one of these animals, but that wasn't Katie's way.

Katie spoke up, "Excuse me. Is there someone that I can talk to about how you keep meetings organized?" There was no sound, and all the Meerkats seemed to have disappeared.

Katie walked closer to the burrows but stayed at least 8-10 feet away so they would feel more comfortable. She repeated her statement. "Excuse me, I don't want to hurt you. I want to find out about meetings. I have seen your work. I thought you might have some information to share. I would like to understand from your vast experience."

One of the Meerkats peeked his head out of the burrow. He looked at the wolf and then disappeared again. Katie sat down, as did Joe and Summer. They knew this was going to be a waiting game for them.

The Meerkats were in their burrow, and the one that had peeked his head out said to another. "Do you think these are the three wolves the zebra's mentioned to us?"

The other said, "I think so. They seem like they want to talk."

Suddenly, three of the group's older members squeezed into the conversation. "Do you want to trust wolves? They are scary."

"But if they are friendly, maybe they can protect us."

"I don't trust anyone but our kind. How can we trust them?" the third Meerkat asked

"There is only one way to find out. I have to go out and see. If I don't come back, we know the answer." The first replied.

The Meerkat that originally had peeked his head out looked again and saw Katie sitting alone. He extended his head slightly to notice the other two wolves sitting behind her with their heads down. They weren't in a stance to attack. He continued to come out of the burrow.

"Did you say meetings? What did you want to know?" The Meerkat asked.

"Hi. I am Katie. My friends and I run a small business building homes. We don't know anything about meetings. We are looking to be more organized. I noticed that you were all working together. I had hoped you could share what you do to keep your group organized."

"Are you the one that talked to the zebras?"

Katie said, "No, my friend Summer did." Katie motioned to Summer. Summer raised a paw to wave.

The Meerkat was still cautious but a little more comfortable. "Meetings are when a group of us get together to discuss a certain topic. We find the topic that needs to be discussed and ensure all the relevant animals are together for the conversation."

The Meerkat was thinking about a recent meeting they had yesterday. They had to discuss who would live in a new burrow they were building on the far side of the field. This new burrow was three times larger than any others they currently occupied. There would be lots of interest in moving there even though it didn't connect with the other burrows yet. More extensive burrows allowed them more food storage and more places to move around during the colder months. The Meerkats had a group of diggers working on connecting the two burrows, but they still needed several months to accomplish this. The meeting gave the head of each of the families a turn to speak about who they thought would be the best to occupy the new burrow. Each family head understood not to say anything while the others talked and listened to their thoughts or concerns.

The person leading the meeting was our head digger. This digger had been making these burrows for years. They are a respected part of the community who consistently were able to listen to all sides of a discussion and then determine a reasonable solution. With this situation, he had decided that two families would move to the new burrow. One who was older with several slower-moving Meerkats. The second family has many younger members that could quickly go between the burrows. The head digger felt this was fair to all until the connection between the burrows was completed. Once completed, the whole community would have a large area, but he didn't want to leave it empty until then. If he left it empty, it could be taken by other animals, such as snakes, who wish to use their work.

Katie said, "Are there specific types of ways you conduct your meetings to ensure you can get the desired results?"

The Meerkat was intrigued; this wolf was asking and was generally interested in how they conducted their meetings. This was a complicated answer since meetings had many different types, but the Meerkat needed to focus on three meetings. He wanted to focus on a standard leader-led, brainstorming, and stand-up meeting. He thought those would illustrate the point effectively that this wolf could use these as a basis for her developing her style. Meetings were all about style. Your way of setting the scope, direction, and facilitating makes all the difference. The Meerkat had seen over the years that some of his elders had chosen to enter the meeting with a heavy-handed style that just focused on giving orders to get things done. It was adequate, but it also lost the ability to gain respect from others in the community. His fellow Meerkats in the community would only go because they had to attend, not because they felt their contribution was necessary. This was something he felt was always missing from his elder's perspective. Why would he have a meeting that community members were forced to attend that would never be effective? They would never learn how to work together when a problem arose and the elder wasn't around to give them a solution.

The Meerkat realized he was thinking in his head instead of saying something out loud.

"The first important part of any meeting is the goal. If you don't have a goal, it's a waste of time to meet. Over the years, I have seen different community groups get together and start talking. They think it's a meeting, but it's just a get-together without any specific reason except to complain and talk. That is not a meeting."

Katie said, "So that I understand you correctly, you are saying that getting together and talking is not a meeting?"

"Correct, from my point of view, a meeting has to be a group of the community that gets together to discuss an issue toward collaborating to meet a goal. An example of an issue might be that one of the tunnels is blocked in the burrow. An example of a goal would be finding a place to get a constant secondary water supply. These may involve multiple community members, so we will meet to discuss how each member could contribute."

Katie thought momentarily before asking questions since she wanted to get this straight in her head. There must be an objective for a meeting to occur. Other times, you're just getting together to talk. That was an interesting idea that she hadn't thought about in that way. Sometimes, she talks to a group about a house design, but it's not really to accomplish a task. It's just talking. Sometimes, she is just brainstorming with her colleagues. There are times Katie is talking to hear about her colleagues' lives. It may seem like a meeting, but it never is, it's just people talking.

"That makes sense." Katie replied.

"Now let's consider a different leader-led meeting. The leader organizes a leader-led meeting to get updates or talk with his team. I lead this meeting by coming in with a few agenda items to share with my team. Then, I go around the room to ask for three things they should share with the group. I am not asking for details here because I usually hear details in individual sessions if needed. The example that comes to mind is the tunnel blocked in the burrow. This occurred a few months ago when a cave-in occurred. We couldn't easily dig the dirt out of the way because the blockage expanded and could cause stability problems in other parts of the burrow. My friend called a meeting of the diggers, designers, and leaders to discuss what occurred and how it could be repaired. The leader was able to get everyone together." The Meerkat recounted the meeting.

He started the meeting by saying, *Thank you all for coming. As you may or may not know, we have a blocked cave in Burrow Thirty-eight that stops traffic between that and Burrow Twenty-eight. We attempted to dig out the secure area, but the burrow wouldn't stay up because other burrow parts started to collapse. I am looking to you to help solve this problem.*

He then turned to his left and said this is the digger on the job. *Do you have anything to add?*

The digger replied, *We are looking for alternative solutions since when we tried to use our usual method of keeping the tunnel clear with mud and leaves, it didn't work due to the looseness of the dirt in that area.*

The leader said, *Does anyone else have ideas?*

The meeting collected input from several groups on how to proceed with digging a new cave, moving dirt from one place or another, and even abandoning that section without a connection between the burrows. The meeting concluded with the leader spending lots of time listening to the suggestions.

The leader continued,. *Thank you for your input, but we all know how vital this connection is for our way of life. I want us to explore and build an alternative path around the broken section. Once we have that path open, I will call this group to discuss our plans for the damaged area.*

The meeting concluded, and the leader sat alone, but he took some notes on the discussion and results. The leader knew the next step was to get the key people back together tomorrow to look at all the suggestions and see which ideas they could try.

The Meerkat said, "This was how one leader ran his meeting. It meets the objectives we discussed."

"That's a good conclusion by the leader."

"Yes, that is how meetings are supposed to work. They don't always work that way, though," The Meerkat said under his breath.

The Meerkat sat there, looking out at the world at that statement. He knew that was how he had hoped all meetings would go, but inevitably, some meetings have everyone talking without accomplishing anything. He knew he worked hard to avoid discussions unraveling into that whenever possible.

"Setting the direction to solve the problem was essential in that meeting. Restating the problem helps energize your community and ensures that everyone knows what to do. I prefer these types of meetings because they are direction focused. Please know that sometimes leaders can't decide on a course of action after one discussion. This is because it can have complex dependencies that need to be considered. When this occurs, a leader needs more time to make a decision. I have left these meetings unsatisfied, But I have been around long enough with our leadership to know they will discuss the issue again and come back to us. I love the back-and-forth that our leadership does. It allows for more input even when deciding which decisions to make because it keeps everyone who wants to be included involved."

The Meerkat took a breath, then continued, "We have had leaders in the past that would leave a meeting without taking any questions. They would leave lots of confusion since questions will be unanswered. A few days later, they would decide without telling us. It was frustrating; we would see many community members complaining. This wasn't productive, and everything was always delayed primarily because no one wanted to work on the project since they didn't feel a part of it. What I have learned about teams, even if a leader makes a decision that someone doesn't agree with, if they had an opportunity to be heard, they are more likely to support a decision. We found in our community a back-and-forth exchange in the decision process to be effective toward getting results. A leader-led meeting can be extremely effective for building a collaborative culture."

Katie sat there smiling. She was getting the concept and was reassured that it only sometimes works out. She knew this would happen to the three wolves being young leaders. For her team in the business, it would only be a matter of time until things go differently than they expected. She hoped that she could steer the team back to the right course. She wondered how this could be accomplished.

"How would you steer the community back to the right path if they are complaining and not meeting expectations." Katie asked.

"That's a big question that involves teamwork, meetings, culture, and failure. Let's focus on meetings, and in the future, we can talk about some of those other topics." The Meerkat replied.

The Meerkat paused momentarily, then turned around since he thought he heard something. He looked around and saw a few of the younger Meerkats staring at him from one of the burrows a little farther away. They were sent to check to see if he had gotten eaten. He smiled at how nice the whole community looked out for each other. This can't be taught; it is just understood in the Meerkat community. Everyone is in this for the community rather than themselves.

The Meerkat said, "Excuse me a minute." He turned and then ran down to one of the burrows. Katie watched him since she thought she saw something pop its head out but wasn't sure what this Meerkat was doing.

The Meerkat returned a few minutes later. The Meerkat said, "My apologies; they checked on me to ensure I wasn't eaten."

Katie was in shock, "Eaten! Why would I?"

She realized she was a wolf before she could finish her statement. She had a Meerkat meal with her parents a long time ago. It was not unheard of for her old pack to eat Meerkats. They were easy to catch if you were patient.

Katie continued, "Oh. I understand." She was feeling sad

about the way of the world at that moment. She may have been the dominant animal, but it didn't mean she knew everything. There are others like the Meerkats that run communities better than their old pack.

"Please explain how you get your community back toward the correct goal. This is very interesting." Katie asked,

"Sure. The best way to get the community back on the right goal is to set out the problem and let them talk about it. The method that the first leader did wasn't only looking for input from others in the community. It was making the problem not only his issue but also making the issue a community problem. When we make a problem something everyone has to solve, it becomes part of them. It's their responsibility. When an animal feels responsible for it, they will work harder to ensure the issue is resolved. No matter if they are part of the solution or not. They take pride in the solution because it was their joint problem. When it's just the leader's problem, fewer people care about it, even if it affects them. They think it's someone else's issue to solve. Sharing it with everyone gives the whole community a sense of ownership, which generates pride in the solution. When we have established this in our community, our members will go out of their way to ensure everyone comes together to offer assistance. This is how we keep the community on track if they get sidetracked."

"Thank you. This was helpful." Katie was thinking about this. How would she build a sense of community and pride within the business? This was part of the Meerkat's makeup, which was crucial for their work.

The Meerkat was trying to figure out why a wolf that is all-powerful and can hunt for anything it wanted consider these little things helpful to her.

"Of course, but why is this helpful?"

Katie said, "Our business is to make homes for animals in

the forest and other places. At times we can't get ourselves organized. I am looking for ideas on how to keep the team going in the right direction."

"That makes sense, definitely organized meetings can help achieve this goal. Have you ever considered a brainstorming meeting?"

"A brainstorming meeting, what's that?" Katie asked and looked surprised. She had never heard of such a thing.

"A brainstorming meeting is a meeting where the objective is to generate lots of ideas that the group can consider before they choose a few to try out. This type of meeting is very effective when you want multiple ideas to solve a problem. We all know that solving a problem doesn't have to be solved in one way. We have seen leaders that say do it one way or another, but they don't consider all the alternatives."

The Meerkat took a breath, "For example, there is never one way to clear the ground for building a new burrow. You could use your paws to wipe it, pull the grass, eat the grass, and have another animal do it for you. We may not like some of these solutions, but many alternatives exist. When we organize a brainstorming meeting, we get a group of the community from different areas to offer a variety of perspectives. Multiple perspectives allow us to hear solutions we have yet to think about. We go out into the community to find who may have knowledge on the subject. We aren't looking for only all subject matter experts, instead, we seek community members with desire and passion who can offer unique but reasonable ideas. We get the new group together to meet and then state the problem without jargon. We ask everyone to come up with at least five ideas. We tell them there are no bad ideas in this room."

Katie interrupted, "No bad ideas. What does that mean?"

"Yes, it's a method we use to allow them to think by being free. We need to remember parents always want their young to do better than them. To do this, they can stifle their movements until they learn the correct way to complete tasks. This stops some freedom of expression which we are eliminating to find great ideas."

"That makes sense."

The Meerkat continued, "We ask everyone to present their ideas. We allow each one to share, and sometimes duplicate ideas are presented. This is fine for us because every idea isn't always the same. After all the sharing we work to eliminate the ideas that aren't doable. Like the idea of having another animal clear the land, who do we know that we could ask to clear the land? We realized we didn't know anyone to help us."

The Meerkat took a breath, and his seriousness turned to a smile.

"The best part of this brainstorming meeting is that each person involved can go back to their area of the community. They share their ideas and gain feedback. Each part of our community can hear the ideas to see if there is something important that wasn't considered. The team member then brings the ideas back to the main group. A long list of alternatives is generated for the team leader. They can try out a few based on the feedback received. It's really helpful having everyone share since we find lots of great ideas."

"Astonishing. You really get a group involved. How successful have these projects been?"

"Extremely successful, lots in the community have volunteered to help. I have even met other Meerkats from a different community, who visited to pitch in with a project. When I asked them how they heard about this and why they wanted to be involved, they said they were at one of their friend's houses in our community when we were sharing ideas. They could contribute to the ideas when they heard about the project. They felt coming back to help would be worthwhile and have met lots of new friends. It goes back to when people got off track, leaders need to help. Our way is bringing them back together on a project."

Katie asked, "Is this a quick process if you gather input from others outside of the initial meeting?"

"Nope, it takes a long time. This process could take months to get to a unified plan. With any large-scale projects, you need to think big and spend time considering all the options. It's always better to take your time than rush and have to reverse course. If it's something that needs to be decided quickly this type of meeting won't work."

"Wow. That takes a lot of coordination. I would have to work with my other team leaders to do this effectively." Katie commented.

"Definitely. Please don't rush on this one."

"Thank you. Your meeting ideas have been so helpful. I appreciate you taking some of your valuable time to spend with me today." Katie turned to leave.

She didn't want to take any more of the Meerkat's valuable time. The Meerkat had taken a long time to explain all of this. Katie felt guilty since she didn't want the other members of their community hiding in the burrow the rest of the day.

"Wait! Where are you going? There is one more piece of information that you need to know," the Meerkat shouted.

Katie turned around. "I didn't want to take up any more of your time. You shared valuable details, but I am sure your community is anxious to get out to enjoy the day."

"The Zebra was right, you are very courteous. There is only one more idea I would like to share. It won't take long," The Meerkat said.

Katie turned and sprinted back toward the Meerkat. The Meerkat had a big smile but almost got run over by Katie when she couldn't stop herself as she ran next to him. She fell to the ground, causing dirt to splash upward like a fog covering the area.

Joe and Summer were back in the brush. They looked up and laughed as Katie was lying on the ground with dirt and mud all over her face.

"Are you ok?"

"Yes." She stood up and walked back a few steps while shaking everything off.

"The last meeting I want to share is called the stand up or lunch meeting. Both meetings involve getting everyone together for an update on how the project is progressing. Progressing isn't the right word; it's more about hearing how each piece of a project is going. When we don't talk to each other about the different parts of a project things start to fall apart. We have seen this occur with the burrow project I mentioned. We had teams digging from each side, but one group was not talking to the other group. So initially they were digging on two opposite sides of the caved-in tunnel. This wasn't making any forward progress. We were getting nowhere to fix the broken tunnel. We implemented these stand-up meetings which are quick. We asked one question, 'How is progress going?' and everyone shares. This is effective for communication in groups fast. The style has been used since my parents' days, it's effective."

"I like quick. I am not a patient wolf." Katie has always had a problem sitting still. This type of meeting would help her get information and go on to the next task.

The Meerkat laughed, "This is perfect for you then. In a short period you can get specific details."

"Wait but where does lunch come in?" Katie asked.

"Oh, I forgot. Lunch meetings are similar to this but usually we start with a meal. The beginning of any meeting where people eat, somehow it breaks down barriers, then members of the team begin to talk. We find this effective when there is a disagreement among community members. But bringing food to a meeting the issues that were prevalent, no longer matter. These are designed to be quick and effective in finding the core issue then solving it."

"You're right that was quick."

"One more detail you need to know. You have to be flexible with everything. If you see something happening in a meeting that is working, let it flow. If the flow goes off too far, I use this tool called an idea board. This is a place where when we have an off topic idea or an off topic conversation, we take it and add it to the board. We then refocus on what is occurring in the meeting. Does that make sense?" The Meerkat asked.

"Yes, the idea board is a place to hold ideas while you focus on the original conversation. Right?"

"Exactly. Do you understand all of what I shared?"

Katie was overwhelmed; she had just gotten all this information, but how would she explain it to her two friends and then, even worse, implement it.

"I think so, there is a lot to go over. I am not sure I will know how to implement all this."

The Meerkat replied, "Good!" His voice was loud and commanding. Katie almost jumped back.

"I would be sad if you had said you understand everything right away. These things take time and practice. I have given you tools and a starting point. It's up to you to figure out how you will put it into practice. Remember, try one thing then another, don't try it all right away." The Meerkat said.

"Can I come back to ask follow up questions?"

The Meerkat laughed, "Anytime but hopefully not too soon." He didn't want to deal with the scared community who would not want to come out of their burrows. The rest of the Meerkats would be worried about a wolf coming to their home regularly. He would have to reassure them that these were friendly wolves.

The Meerkat disappeared into his burrow.

Katie said at his disappearing back, "Thank you so much. I can't believe you spent so much time talking to me. I really know this will help a lot."

Katie knew this was all she would get from him. She had many questions, like where she would start, how she would describe meetings, and whether they were any different than a conversation she would have with Joe or Summer. Her mind was going a mile a minute, but she knew this would take time to settle it. She had no idea what she would say to them as she turned to walk back to where Joe and Summer were sitting. It was like she had just forgotten everything she knew and sat down.

Summer spoke up first, "You look exhausted?"

"I am, I felt like they just gave me so much information that my brain is going to explode." Katie replied.

"It's ok Katie, you can tell us when you are ready to share. We could walk for a bit? I would like to get to that out cropping over there before the evening." Joe pointed to a rock formation at least an hour's walk.

Summer and Katie nodded and began walking.

Summer said, "I was thinking that we should bring together more people into our team."

Katie said, "Our group here or to help with the building team?"

"The building team, I like our leadership pack just the three of us for now."

Katie said, "I agree, with all we are learning it may be better to have some help with all the building. Then we can ensure we deliver quality work."

"Exactly."

They were at the base of the rock; Joe circled and found a way to the top. They followed Joe, and the view from here was breathtaking; you could see the whole landscape that surrounded this area. They were as high as the treetops, allowing them to see the dense forest off to one side. Luckily for them, a pool of water had collected on the side of the rock. They all needed to quench their thirst.

They sat down to rest for the evening. Katie began to talk about what she learned.

"There are three meetings that we need to implement a leader lead meeting, a brainstorming meeting and a lunch meeting. Once we have these implemented correctly some of our problems should end."

Katie explained in detail about the meetings. They knew this was great information, but they had to figure out how to use it in their business. Neither knew the answer, but they knew it would come to them. They fell asleep as the sun set on the horizon.

ANTS

They had journeyed back home to absorb all that they had learned. Katie and Summer went inside.

Joe was sitting outside his house looking at this large organization chart. There are teams of builders who construct the homes, designers who talk to the clients, searchers who find supplies, finance people who handle the payments, and managers who oversee the project timelines.

House building involved each of these teams. The teams needed to understand how their contribution was part of the business. He hoped by doing this, he could work on improving communication, trust, and empowerment. He had no idea on how to start this. If he could figure this out, it would be the last part of their journey in team leadership.

Joe didn't know where to turn to find this answer, but he knew he could figure this out. He looked around, hoping that an idea would appear.

He saw a line of Ants walking up a tree to his right. He didn't pay too much attention to them. He focused more on the ants carrying a big log in front of him, walking across the grass. He waved to them, and they waved back. They continued on their way to their home.

To his left, there was a small mound coming out of the ground. He noticed two lines of ants going into the mound. He wondered how these ants kept themselves so organized. He thought that the ants must be constantly communicating. He was sure they knew the other aspects of leadership which are trust, empowerment, and growth. He had hoped they could share with him their knowledge.

Joe told one of the ants, "Excuse me, I am Joe. Is there someone I can ask about team leadership?"

The ants all scattered in different directions as if they were scared of him. Joe could imagine this: an enormous wolf talking to them. Joe stood there; no ants returned. He decided to put his head down to wait.

He waited for a long while until one ant put his head out.

"Excuse me but is there someone I can talk to?"

The little ant looked up at this wolf lying in the grass, just sitting there. "Let me check, but please don't squash us!" Before disappearing into the mound.

A few minutes later, the Ant appeared with another ant. They looked at Joe. They said nothing; the ants just stood there for a few moments. One ant shook his head at the other, then both left. Joe could not distinguish each ant from the other, so he couldn't tell if it was the same Ant or others.

Joe lay there for a few more moments, and then two more ants appeared.

They went on to a high leaf to look at Joe.

Chris, one of the ants, "Hi, I am Chris. I am responsible for leading the workers. This is Paul, he is responsible for ensuring we have enough items to live. How can we assist you?"

"I have been watching you for some time. I noticed the

Ant's in your community go together in a line, I often wondered how you communicate?"

"I don't think that communication is your question. I think you really want to know something else?" Chris replied.

"I really want to have my teams communicate so they can figure out things without asking every time there is an issue."

"It's all about the culture that you set for your organization. Are you the leader?" Chris asked.

"Yes, I am the leader of the team."

"Well, it's up to you to set the expectations that everyone in the organization will follow. When you go out, people look at you. If they see you helping out then they will help out without asking. If your employees don't feel like they can do anything without your say they have a reason for doing that. Possibly they had received direction from you or others in leadership that made them feel like they should wait before proceeding. The waiting for them to be told the next step is because they have been educated to follow this behavior. Do you do this?" Chris replied.

"We don't do that, at least I think," Joe knew he didn't do that, but he did realize that parts of the organization did this. "I have to change this practice. My plan has been to tell people the end goal. This would allow them to focus more on building the home, our final product."

"Exactly that is the first step to empowerment; it's telling your team where you want to go, then you can give them some incremental steps to reach the goal. I have always learned from our culture that we never tell all the steps to the goal. We will lay out a process that helps promote positivity. Each team and individual have to learn how to get to the goal through trial and error."

"Learn it themselves? Really?"

"Exactly, you want your staff to feel like they are making a difference. If they can't figure something out without a leader, how are they going to take the initiative?" Chris stated.

Joe was staring at Chris in wonder. Chris was saying what he needed to hear. He needed his people to feel empowered to do the work without him. Joe was feeling more burned out lately. He was fielding many simple questions recently while his mind had to concentrate on finances and future goals. All of this was putting the world's weight on his shoulders and not giving him the room to empower his staff.

Joe understood what Chris meant. When he was thrown out of his pack, he had to figure out things on his own. The Mountain Goat had taught Joe to look at things from different perspectives. Joe was in the middle of the mountains with snow all around, but he was dying of thirst. He didn't know where to find water. The Mountain Goat gave him simple advice: 'Drink plenty of fluids. Snow is good.' He didn't know what that meant at first, but he figured it out. Joe knew he had to do this in the organization for them to develop.

"You need to let your team know that you trust them, and they can do the job by doing this you are empowering them to complete the task. It doesn't matter if it's the right or wrong way, just that the task is completed to the customer's satisfaction. I have seen a lots of way for ants to find food. There are always faster and slower ways, but does it matter as long as they come back with food?"

"It doesn't matter? Really? We have always followed a process." Joe was confused because, in his experience, the process mattered.

Chris replied, "It doesn't matter when you focus on the end goal. We need to remember that we are here to help our team develop. Communication is an important aspect, but without empowering, you will never get the most out of your team."

Joe knew this was the true statement. He had to empower

his staff and let them figure it out. He knew it wouldn't all go right initially, but he had to take the first step.

He remembered a situation when he was in a pack with his mom years ago. His father, Caesar, was annoyed at a few other wolves in the pack when they didn't secure a meal for them that evening. He said, "It's OK to fail. By not catching that deer for dinner, what did you learn about what happened today?" The wolves who scared off their dinner said, "We were too noisy and that chased away the deer. We were also head strong since we thought we could do anything. We didn't take time to remember what you taught us about patience is a benefit when hunting, since the prey is always moving, but we can wait for them to come to us."

Joe was thinking about the 'OK to fail' that Caesar used with his pack. If his team felt it was 'OK to fail', he could institute a celebration when the workers developed a new method to a problem. That would bring about new ideas and fix some of the issues. Joe knew he would want to modify Caesar model to 'OK to fail forward.' This meant to Joe that anyone trying a new idea and fails it would be alright, as long as they learn from what occurred they were failing forward. When they did this, they could be rewarded. We have to help our teams try new things when they are stagnant and not achieving their potential.

Joe turned to Chris to say, "Empowerment is letting people know it's alright if failure occurs too."

"Of course, failure is a natural process of any team. Too many times ants don't get along with each other so then one asks to work for a different team. Our community doesn't see this as a bad thing, just a steppingstone until we find the right ant to take their place. You should do something similar, since with the right culture there are always opportunities for your staff to move between teams."

"Do you think Empowerment is the first step?"

"I think so. For us we can't be everywhere that has workers collecting different supplies. We found that letting them solve issues when they are a long way away, they have higher morale and able to complete tasks easily," Chris replied.

Joe knew that this empowerment was the step he needed to implement in his business.

"You mentioned trust; how does the ant colony implement this within your teams?"

"We have different viewpoints in the colony but for me trust is the idea that anyone of the ants in this community could be my friend. We have teams working in all different directions of our colony. When we are making a decision in the direction where food can be found, I bring all my team leads together for a discussion. The discussion leads to two directions, and I tell them to pursue the directions you chose. I trust their knowledge of the surrounding area to find the best possible sources. This trust always builds upon itself since they feel ownership in making decisions."

After licking his antenna, he continued, "Trust is the key part of our culture as a team. I have seen a team succeed or fail based on trust. We have implemented a project that requires multiple teams to collectively work together. If the project is delayed because a specific team doesn't complete a task. The associated teams begin to lose trust in that team. If this occurs multiple times, the teams will lose trust in leadership and could spiral through the colony. We try to not have this happen, teams get delayed, but we try to pitch in whenever possible. It has caused some morale issues, but we try to smooth any emotions out when they occur. A team doing other's work is never good. To avoid this, our goal is to ensure all ants are successful. We work with our teams to build up relationships of trust across all teams. Which allows others to empathize with what is happening across the colony."

"Wow, that is great that teams will help out each other. Do you train them to do different jobs?"

Chris continued, "Sometimes but everyone wants to help. We work to build trust in a way that everyone is included. Trust for us, is built at the team. When a new member wants to join a team, we give them tasks to complete on their own time. We want to see if they care enough to accomplish the tasks in additional to their normal duties. If they complete the tasks, they will have passed our tests, and we assign them to the team. If they can't complete the tasks, we will send them back to get more learning. We encourage them to try harder and tell them they have opportunities to try again. We feel that all ants have a place in our organization. We find where each has expertise then place them on the right team."

Joe said, "This sounds like leadership?"

"It's not leadership specifically it's how we help each Ant find their path. Each of us has our path in our colony. Some ants know their place from when they are young. Others need help to find their place. We give each one the opportunities for peer mentoring to shadow others and learn what is performed on each team. This in turn builds trust for the new mentees as they learn all the complex parts of the colony. We build trust with the individual ants early, then teams are always successful."

Joe knew what Chris just shared was the key that he had to implement to make his teams succeed. The process of just having everyone follow each other would be a challenge. He needed to help his staff find their path in the company. He had found his path through trial and error. It led him to build a team with Katie and Summer. Trust was developed for them by going through shared experiences. The same is needed for the staff in the company.

"Is trust something you build individually, or do you do this on teams?" Joe asked.

Chris said, "We build trust through a positive reinforcement model which focuses on developing the person and in turn it develops the team."

Paul, the other ant sitting there, had not said anything.

He finally spoke up, "When we develop the individual ant, we know their different expertise. We ensure all teams have a diverse set of skills on a team. The diverse skills allow the team to have different roles contributing to the objective. When we are sharing the objective, we tell the whole team. This prevents any one person from being pigeonholed to only doing their role, each Ant can contribute to different roles if needed. We made more mistakes when we had only given each Ant a specific role."

Joe said, "Mistakes, that is what we have been having. I am looking for ways to help avoid this. Can you give me an example of something that happened and how you fixed it?"

"Sure. We found when ants rush, they cause problems in the colony," Paul thought for a minute before speaking. "We collect supplies for the winter. We sent a team to collect willow leaves to use for beds. Instead of collecting willow leaves the team collected maple leaves that are delicious but not good for beds. By the time we noticed, it was too late because we were already underground for the winter without enough beds. The only solution was to give two maple leaves for beds, it wasn't perfect, but we made do. When we asked the team that collected the maple leaves what happened. They said it was faster to collect the closest leaves for beds, than walking to the willow tree. This team was focused on completing the goal quickly, they didn't consider all the consequences. It wasn't a horrible mistake, but it affected the colony. We decided that going forward that we focused on accuracy rather than doing tasks quickly."

Joe sat in the grass but didn't say anything. He was wondering if he had team members doing this. There are ways he could do things quickly; he asked himself if this type of work had caused some of the recent mistakes. He was thinking about the house on the hill. It needed additional support so it would be more stable standing on the mountain. Instead, the team built a flat home without the supports, which would not be secure for that location. He knew this was a mistake due to rushing, but they had to fix it before anyone could live in the house.

Joe asked, "How would you avoid this issues like the maple leaves in the future?"

"We decided that we would focus on quality. To ensure we get the right materials, even if it takes us longer. Since then we haven't ever had the wrong leaves for the winter again."

Joe knew that quality was the correct answer but wondered if there was more to trust and communication.

"Is trust and communication linked?" Joe asked

"Yes, in our colony we communicate easily by ensuring everyone knows the objectives. We share all the details, even when things change. We reshare everything." Chris replied,

"What do you mean you share when things change? We share information with staff, but it's never completely understood."

"It's easy and difficult at the same time specifically for us. It easy for us since we tell our leaders, and they are responsible for communicating it to the teams. These teams are about ten ants or less. This ensures everyone knows their leader, who they communicate with regularly and it's easy to share changes in objectives." Chris replied.

"How are you sure that it's communicated, within organizations managers don't always communicate everything."

"It depends on the culture of your organization. We have instituted a culture of sharing that everyone values. By doing this everyone feels connected, sharing is commonplace for us."

Joe understood that culture was something that he needed to develop within his teams.

Joe asked Paul, "If someone steps out of line, how do others not step out of line?"

Paul said, "It's all communication. Each ant has a buddy that is in front or behind them, they tell them through hand signals or verbally. The ants are all taught to use both interchangeably which allows them to communicate in all situations."

"Hand signals, wait! You don't really have hands, only legs."

"It's more like nods and taps with our legs. We have developed a sort of language that allows us to understand each other. It is vital for us. A few years ago, Peter developed the hand signals when he was trying to communicate between teams on different trees. Peter taught other teams, they loved it, and adopted it quickly. Then we added it to our learning program." Paul replied.

Joe looked baffled by Paul's statement about a learning program.

Paul continued, "When an ant is ready to join a team you need to spend at least a month learning the specific processes and customs. We have found teams that are successful when they form standard practices to communicate. In the worker team they use a term called LIP whenever there is an obstacle in the way. It is short for 'Log In Path that needs to be moved,' but it applies to anything that is blocking their way to the destination. It is quick, easy, and allows the message to get across to the whole team so they know they have an obstacle that has to be cleared quickly. By using an acronym problems are quickly shared. We also use names for different entrances and exits. This allows us to know where to go in and out of the colony."

"Names? You name your doors. Don't you just use 1, 2, 3 or

4. I know that is what we call our area's 1, 2, 3, or 4. depending on where you need to work." Joe said

Paul wanted to laugh, but he knew that Joe was still learning and didn't want to offend him.

Paul continued, "Using names instead allows us to easily identify the entrances and exits. We discovered that when we used numbers, ants kept putting the numbers in order. That is good for always counting the correct number of leaves collected but not for entrances. We found ants don't understand when we say, 'today we are using entrance 8' and that is next to 14, when 14 was the most recent entrance built so it was named that way. Our colony was totally confused. It caused all kinds of backups, so we realized early on in our development to name our entrances and exits."

"What are the names?"

"We asked the team leaders to come up with an overall category that was broad enough that we could have countless names. The team leaders came up with two we liked, which were flowers and places. We chose places then named entrances/exits Maple, Jasmine, Evergreen, Brick, etc. These are places that have meaning to the entire colony." Paul replied.

Joe was getting it. He knew this would be helpful to his team.

"Thank you for describing names." Joe sat for a minute before asking his next question.

"Do you ever find miscommunication between different groups such as between the diggers and workers ants."

Paul laughed and interrupted Chris, "All the time."

Chris said, "Last week the digger ants took down one of the main tunnels we use to collect supplies. They didn't let anyone know, at least the leaders thought they didn't. There were lines of ants waiting inside that couldn't get out. The ants were all frustrated. I ended up talking to the leader of the team. The digger team had sent out a message to their leaders about the needed tunnel repair but whoever they told in our leadership had not communicated it down to us. Which was unusual. We had a mess until we told the diggers no one had been told. The diggers realized the dilemma then worked out an alternative way to get out. After the traffic jam was resolved, I had a talk with my leaders. It seems they were informed but ignored it at the time, since they had gotten numerous messages about tunnel work recently. They thought they had communicated it to their teams multiple times but they didn't realize this was new information."

Chris breathed and said, "I didn't say it to them, but this will be a big problem for us if our leaders don't read what other teams are doing in detail. It could easily cause more delays for supplies and bring down the morale of the colony. I want to ensure communication between leaders is more effective. I plan to meet after our talk to break down these silos and enhance communication."

"How will you go about breaking down the silos you mentioned?" Joe asked.

"I planned to talk with the ants on the digger team at the higher levels to ask them to include me on the communications. I will then meet with the leaders on our team, to discuss what was missed in the communication. In the discussion, I will ask them how can the messaging be improved so our relationship with the digger team stays strong."

Joe said, "Yes, communicate between your silo's that's important. Do you always have to go up the chain and back down to get the message out?"

"Unfortunately, that has been our internal structure, but it isn't working. I am trying to propose an alternative solution, similar to what we communicate colony wide with hand signals and acronyms."

Joe knew he had seen this exact issue recently. The silos were not communicating, and that was causing other mistakes. "The key to empowering your colony is to focus on the trust and communication you built?"

Chris replied, "Yes, it's the focus, even with these silos it's the steps we need to make us work together."

"Thank you to you both."

Chris and Paul both said, "You're Welcome. Come back anytime."

Joe turned and walked away. He had more answers than he expected. His mind was racing with all the information the ants shared. He didn't know precisely how to implement all these lessons, but he knew if he had the passion and drive to conquer them.

TEAM MEETINGS IMPLEMENTATION

Katie was impatient; she wanted to take some of the lessons she learned from meeting with the Meerkats and implement them. Katie was designing a house, but it wasn't going well. She knew she needed to work with the scavengers team to find suitable wood. She had to figure out a way to have them work together.

Instead of waiting to make a plan with Joe and Summer, she decided to pull together her best scavengers.

She asked three of the raccoons and three of the squirrels to meet for a discussion. The raccoons, where their night eyes could see in the pitch black, could always see wood that would help them. The squirrels she had recruited were the daytime team that was always busy from sunrise to sunset. Collecting supplies and spotting wood was easy for them.

The objective was to have them communicate better about how to locate the trees they marked in their search. There had been issues with finding the trees these teams marked in their travels. She had sent staff to collect trees, but when they arrived at the spot, they couldn't find the trees. This was causing some difficulty in keeping up their goals.

Katie thought they could devise solutions if she could get these scavengers together. Picking a bare spot in the forest where a few rocks littered the area gave everyone a good view of each other.

"Thank you all for coming. I know it's late for the squirrels and early for the raccoons but I truly appreciate you taking the time."

She always thought it was better to complement them before discussing. Choosing twilight, which was not ideal for either team member ensured that one member didn't think she was favoring another.

She continued, "We have been having some trouble locating the wood from your scavenger missions. We sent a team out two days ago to a couple of the spots you identified but they only came back with broken pieces of wood. I know there is wood that you spotted out there but how do we better identify the locations?"

The raccoon said, "It's not our fault, it's the collectors. If they follow our lead, we can direct them to exactly where the trees are located."

Katie replied, "We aren't here to cast blame on anyone, we know that you are doing great work. We wouldn't have been able to make as many houses without you. We truly appreciate what you do, our goal here is to focus on how we make improvements."

"Thank you for explaining. I thought you called us here because we did something wrong. We seem to get blamed for stuff we didn't do. Especially when we do the searching and scavenging when everyone is sleeping."

The raccoon turned to his two mates and said, "Remember that time we got blamed for knocking down the beaver's logs, when it was a bear that was hungry turning over everything for a meal."

Another raccoon responded, "Yes, but we didn't get blamed for those three garbage pails we scavenged for an appetizing meal."

The other raccoon replied, "Ya, remember how we got away with it. The store owners blamed those humans. Hahaha."

"We are focused on how to make improvements, it's great to hear about your adventures. Can we do it at another time so we can stay focused on this conversation."

The squirrel said quietly, "We sometimes have trouble identifying where the tree is located. We don't know how to give you a specific location so others can find it."

The squirrels were always the quiet team. They focused on their objectives and were never interested in making noise. They would like to go about their work collecting for the winter without anyone noticing them.

Katie said, "That's understandable. Can we brainstorm a way that would be easier? The only idea I had was putting rocks near the location."

The lead raccoon interrupted, "ROCKS? Huh. Why can't we just say it's four trees off the lake? Your team should be able to locate it."

Katie said, "That is true but which four trees? The lake is large oval shape. We may be starting off on the opposite side of the lake. We wouldn't know which four trees from the lake and where on the road to collect them."

"ROAD!!. That's the dangerous side, why would you ever go over there!"

Another raccoon spoke up, "You make a good point; we think the roadside is dangerous, but others may not."

Katie said, "What about the rock idea? Could we put a rock down by the trees you identify that would be good?"

"I am not sure how we would carry a rock."

A second squirrel said, "Well, we could put rocks down in the area we are looking then move them if we find something."

"Yes, that could work if there was a central pile that we could use. I just don't want to be carrying a rock around when I am using my paws for other things."

The second squirrel replied, "Sure if we have a small pile of rocks. It might require a little back and forth to the location but that would be easier than carrying a rock around all the time."

The raccoon said, "A rock pile could work but we may need a few piles. We move around, almost never stay in one section of the forest."

The second raccoon wasn't convinced, "How would we identify the rocks, there are so many just lying around?"

The raccoon said, "What if we made them different than the others?"

The squirrel jumped in, "Different. What do you mean?"

The raccoon said, "Well. What if they were a different color?"

Katie sat quietly, listening to the back and forth between them. She was delighted with where this conversation was going. She thought about it; *we could have other team members create different colored rocks.*

Before Katie could say anything, the squirrel jumped in. " Different colors, how would we do that? There is no way we have time to start making rocks of different colors."

Katie spoke up, "There is this red clay that exists near the other side of the forest. We have gotten stuck in it a few times. It makes our paws reddish for a while until it finally washes off. We could have other teams use the clay or other materials we have in storage to make colored rocks. Would that work for you?"

The squirrel said, "That would work but please don't make the rocks too heavy."

The raccoons just acknowledged with a nod of their head.

Katie knew that they had just had a successful solution.

Katie said, "Thank you, we will work on putting this together. I am so glad we were able to discuss the issue and find a solution that would work for us. I am planning on doing this when we have other issues. Would that be ok?"

"This was very informative and collaborative. We would come back." The raccoon said

"I agree, we like being involved." The squirrel said

Katie said, "Great. Let's plan to meet next week at the same time to review the colored rocks."

The teams dispersed into the forest. Each seemed to go in their ways, but Katie just sat there for a few minutes. She wanted to review what had just occurred, but then she heard some noise in the brush just out of sight. She crept into the brush to see what was going on. The second raccoon and the second squirrel were talking in the brush. She couldn't hear what they were saying, but she was delighted that they continued to speak after the conversation.

Katie had hoped that the talking would continue. It was the only way that this would work.

Katie was excited to tell Joe. Joe was delighted that this was the first step in breaking down the silos that existed. This was a small but meaningful step for them.

CONCLUSION

Joe sat with Summer and Katie; he said, "I know Katie started already." He glared at Katie but then gave her a smile. Joe wanted to teach her that having a plan is better than jumping in, but it went well, so he was delighted.

Joe continued, "We have learned so much and I am going to talk with Crane before we implement these changes."

Summer jumped off her chair, "WAIT! You can't talk to her, not after the way she talked to you."

Joe said in a calm, patient voice, "She had a right to be frustrated. I think I can convince her to come back with our new plan. If she comes back, we will know we can get others on board that may have low morale among our teams."

Summer protested, "Joe, she may cause more trouble for us. She can just start telling people that we can't manage, and things may get worse."

Joe said, "You are right, things may get worse, but I like hearing other's ideas. If Crane has ideas that are meaningful we should listen. I love all that we learned from Elephant, Zebras,

Meerkats, and Ants. But we can't implement them all at once. It will take time."

Joe continued, "I have grown and learned that if we are going to make this company a success it has to be about all of us. This includes all staff, leadership, and scavengers. By us all working together we will be better. My first step is reaching out to Crane."

Summer said calmly, "I know hearing others is important. I am just reluctant to cause more problems." She had her head down. She was scared this could affect the three of them.

Joe paused and took Summer's paw. He stared into her eyes and said, "Summer, nothing will change how we care about each other. You two are the most important things in my life."

Joe said, "We are going to work together on this. If Crane will agree to work with our teams it will have a positive influence on our process, and we will all be better for it."

Katie said, "Like the Meerkats, where everyone had a say and gave feedback."

Joe looked at Katie and said, "Exactly. That is why I want to reach out to her."

The END....

SUMMARY

Joe, Katie, and Summer learned some essential lessons in team management. They knew they would have to take their time to implement all they learned, but Katie showed some could be done sooner than later. Joe was a planner and knew their company would improve operations if they did a little at a time. The lessons they learned from each of the groups have left an impact.

Fred the Elephant taught them teams need to understand the clear objectives and what it meant to be successful. To do this, team leaders need to ensure they plow the field, catch the rain, and be a sounding board.

The Zebras taught them storytelling to introduce the company values, learn from the elders who are the teachers of the Zebra community, and be open to new ideas. These would have to be weaved in through the organization at different places.

The Meerkats taught them to organize meetings more effectively with leader-based, brainstorming, and stand-up meetings. By running these meetings this way, the team would be more effective. The meetings needed to be more organized, if they had any meetings at all. Joe and Summer knew they had to learn to run meetings more effectively from Katie.

The Ants taught them how to communicate more effectively by focusing on quality over doing things quickly, trusting their teams, breaking down silos, and empowering them to find the right solutions. This would be the culture that had to be changed in their company.

Each group they met with had different approaches but added valuable leadership ideas. This journey helped them to learn about team management, which may be different for each group, but with the knowledge gained, they can use it to organize their team into a better working unit.

Joe knew he would begin planning to implement the Elephant's three rules. His focus is on building confidence in the team.

Summer planned to ensure they knew the processes and where they came from. Bring specific team members to suggest improvements that would make them more effective.

Katie planned to continue to improve meetings with additional collaborators. She knew other things would fall into place if she could improve meeting communication.

Joe, Katie, and Summer are taking the first step toward a

better organization. Each organization can follow their lead to make changes that would allow them to provide better services to their customers.

Quality over quantity always wins out in the end.

PART TWO
EXPLANATION

From the fable, we learned that teams are an essential aspect of everything we do in our lives, either personally or professionally. To accurately understand these concepts, we must understand how to apply them.

Most managers I have worked with always start with. "I need more time to integrate these lessons into my team because I focus on completing the work." That is true, but our team may be suffering if we don't give that part of our focus. In the technology field, change is constant, so we are constantly dealing with issues that need to be solved. Any change won't happen immediately, but doing nothing will hurt the team. I decided to implement these slowly so the team could embrace ideas and focus on the issues at hand.

· · ·

Just start your plan. Teams are very resilient; as you build upon your ideas, they will work together to create solutions, which will always outpace the individuals doing it alone.

THREE RULES FROM THE ELEPHANT

Fred the Elephant outlined three rules and meeting objectives that all team leaders should implement to avoid micromanagement, but they can be used in countless ways. I will break down each one here to see how we may use them.

PLOW THE FIELD

When we prepare a field for planting, we remove all the rocks, weeds, and grass to ensure the ground has all the nutrients for a successful crop. A team leader should do the same when we start a team project. A good team leader sets out a plan that ensures success by removing any roadblocks from meeting the objectives.

The best way to do this:

- Work with stakeholders to have agreement on what is considered a completed project.

- Before the project starts, ensure you have the appropriate finances to fund the project from start to end.
- Allocate the resources. Ensure that the people needed to work on the project have time allocated on their calendar for this project and eliminate any tasks that may distract them.
- Communicate to customers. Ensure the customers know the timetables and any risks associated with the project.

Many other details exist, but as a team leader, you must ensure you prepare any project. Too many tasks in business are started without prior planning, and they fail. We want to avoid this at all costs.

A team leader who identifies them first will ensure projects are ready to begin.

Removing any roadblocks that might be in the way enables you as a leader to proceed toward the objective. - Plowing the Field

CATCH ALL THE RAIN

Rain is pouring down on a field, and farmers try to catch as much of it as possible to water their fields. The farmers never want to overwater a field because the crops will be washed away if it floods. Expert farmers know they need to divert some water to the fields and others to reservoirs. You must do the same as a leader.

Team projects always have colleagues, stakeholders, partners, and customers asking them to handle more tasks. These additional side projects can overwhelm any team, which makes them never work on the original objectives. These side projects might be other paperwork, budgets, multiple meetings, reports, or additional interactions that should have been planned for in the Plowing the Field stage. I consider all this the rain that comes pouring down on successful teams.

When this rain is pouring on top of the team, they feel like they are being drowned with additional responsibilities. We never want our teams to feel like they are drowning in work. Leaders know that teams need breathing room to explore all the project possibilities. If they spend time with additional work, they can't find creative solutions when needed. Teams need to catch the easy answers (i.e., rebooting your phone) rather than fiddle with the systems for hours because their mind is distracted with useless work.

Great team leaders sort through all the requests to assist the team.

Avoiding this is the key, so the concept of "catching all the rain" is to organize any of the side projects. Prioritizing the specific ones that focus on the objectives and eliminating the ones that are not relevant. This challenging task requires the team leader or designee to be a gatekeeper. The benefit is that the team will be the focus on the objectives. The downside is that the customers may feel that they are being neglected since their side projects are not being worked on.

To ensure customers are addressed, leaders usually have to reallocate resources to handle the requests. Leaders with the new additional resources work on customers' requests, and we find that customer satisfaction and team satisfaction are high.

A leader who is a gatekeeper on requests can funnel the side projects to additional resources and focus a team toward the goals. - Catching the Rain

BE A SOUNDING BOARD

When people are working through ideas, they find it extremely helpful to talk to someone about what is happening to hear alternative ideas. When you talk to a wall, the wall doesn't talk back. It just listens. Silence doesn't help creative or logical thinkers develop strategies that consider all options. As a leader, you need to break the silence for your team.

Teams are focused on completing a task, either fixing a system, teaching information, or developing a new idea that could enhance the company's bottom line. Whatever it is, teams are made up of individuals. We all have different backgrounds and experiences that we bring to our teams. As with any group of people, there are times when individuals handle things differently than others. Not in a wrong way; their work style is just different from others. We as leaders must understand this to help listen when different perspectives don't mesh.

As a leader, you can offer your teams an open-door policy. One where you can allow your staff to reach out to you and to have a discussion. This can be physical or virtual, depending on your structure.

To be that objective sounding board, you, as the leader, must refrain from passing judgment or trying to fix the problem in these conversations. The focus here is to help your people talk about the issues affecting them. During these conversations you should brainstorm ideas to help the individual return to their comfort zone. If there is something apparent that you could do to help them, avoid suggesting it during these sessions. Allow them to reach the conclusions that they see from the interactions.

I had a leader who used a method by Dale Carnegie to ask open-ended questions and actively listen during the conversation. My leader would rephrase statements that I said in our discussions slightly different. This allowed me to hear the information differently, which showed me alternatives I hadn't considered.

Active listening is the ability to focus all your energy on the conversation. Good leaders turn off or silence their phones and hide any emails. They don't have a computer screen or anything else between them and the employee. This demonstrates that they are all in for the conversation. This immediately builds trust and positive endorphins within the team members. They feel that there will be a connection between the leader and them. Leaders with these interactions have high morale in the organizations, and teams constantly outperform objectives.

Leaders need to be sounding boards to gain the trust of their employees. When leaders are closed and self-involved, their employees feel they are not approachable when they need to bounce ideas off someone. This leads to lower morale and a breakdown of communication that can hinder the group from achieving its goals.

Enclosed is an example of a conversation that is open-ended with a father who is acting like a sounding board:

In New York, a boy goes into his father's study and asks, "Dad do you have a minute?"

The Dad turns from his computer and says, "Sure, Son."

"Dad, I have an issue. My friend doesn't want me to study with him anymore."

"Why do you think that has occurred?"

"My friend seemed frustrated after our study session today. He didn't seem to get any work done."

"Did you get any work done?"

"No, I kept talking to him about other things in school. Like the sports team and the changes to all our classes."

"Why were you talking to him about other things?"

"I was upset by these changes, it was not allowing me to focus. By talking to him it helped me too not be nervous about everything."

"Is there anything you can do so this doesn't happen in the future?"

The son was thoughtful, "I guess, I can stop talking about these things and focus on work. Or I can talk to my friend to let him know that I would like to talk about a few things that are bothering me before we study."

"Talking to him about the things that are bothering you would help. Even letting him know might make things more productive."

"Thanks Dad." the son hugged his father, and left the room.

———

In this illustration, we can see that the son just needs to have someone be the sounding board for their discussion. The same is true in any work conversation. Active listening is a skill that responds without passing any judgment on the situation. When acting as sounding boards, leaders can gain trust and empower people to work out solutions more efficiently by focusing on this type of interaction.

With any leader, it takes time to develop these skills, but there is a simple process that can guide you.

The Sounding Board Process:

1. Be Open to Conversations
2. Actively listen
3. Provide open-ended questions that help the team members find solutions

Leaders who allow team members to communicate, actively listen, and provide leading questions in a no-judgement zone. They are giving guidance that will build teams that have high morale and outperform objectives - The Sounding Board.

OBJECTIVES AND SUCCESS CRITERIA

Projects that launch without goals, participants, stakeholders, and success criteria are doomed to failure. Team leaders must find ways to develop a better structure that will give ample opportunity to ensure all team members know what needs to be done and how to meet the objective.

Here is a sample outline that we have found successful for our projects. Enclosed is the resources area you can find a Doc and PDF version for use on your future projects.

Outline:

<Name of the Project>
   <Team Leader>
   <Date>

<Description of the Project>

<Objective> (No more than four sentences, bullets are better)

<Time Line> How long will this take to complete?

<Area's/Departments> For internal projects, write who is on the team; if it's external, include client names here.

<Leaders> - Who are the leaders that support this project?

<Success Criteria> - What five or six bullet points will tell you the project is completed?

<Dependencies/Risk>

- Are there any other things that must be completed before we can succeed? If they exist, document them here.
- Are there risks that may impact meeting the success criteria? Acknowledging them here will help the team know these may be a factor that will affect the outcome.

DESIGN YOUR OWN PHILOSOPHY.

Leaders must work to design their own philosophy. To do this, you must apply the three leadership skills you learned to your career. Here are the questions for you to consider:

———

1. Ask at least two friends what are the things that they see that define you as a person. You are seeking ten words that describe who you are. Write them down here.

2. Use the above list to write down which of these top four words define you. If something needs to be added, add it below.

3. What words that describe your personality. Which of these would you want to usc in hclping othcrs mcct thcir own objcc-tives? List a maximum of three terms.

4. The three words you shared in the previous question are the basis for your leadership philosophy. Consider how these define you and write a one-line statement utilizing the thoughts that resonate with you. This statement is your philosophy.

It will be challenging now, but you will develop it over time. Leadership philosophies help you define your objectives and actions when working with people.

ZEBRA LESSONS

STORYTELLING AND LEARNING

Storytelling/Traditions is a powerful method that leaders use to explain situations effectively.

A process is a way of completing a task; the process is just a set of guidelines that show a person the steps to complete the work. It doesn't provide any value and is almost always forgotten after completing the task. It's not something that stays with them.

On the other hand, a story can stay with a person if it can make an emotional connection that allows the receiver to relate to the characters in the story. The story gives the leader a way of communicating information that can have a deeper meaning than just a process to follow.

The guidelines for stories always revolve around a few characteristics.

1. Always share something that can resonate with the team.
2. Ensure the topic is relatable to the group. If you are meeting with accountants, discuss something about finances. Talking about cars won't relate to everyone in the group. We always must know our audience.
3. Share something genuine. Leaders use personal anecdotes or share something that they are passionate about. The more the listener can feel your emotion, the better they will listen and relate.

Story Example:

I am a passionate person when it comes to movies. I especially like the movie called "The Replacements". One of my favorite scenes is near the end of the film when the football game is on the line. A reporter asked him what does the team needs to be successful. The coach says, "Heart". We have all struggled in the last few months with increased costs and low morale. I have never let that stop me from looking at the bright side of every situation. Each one of you are the heart of this team. I wouldn't be here without you, and I wouldn't want to do this job without you beside me. Thank you for always being there through thick and thin.

This story will resonate and be remembered because it lets his team know how important they are to the leader but also relates what he is saying to the movie he liked. You have to find your examples that mean something to you and can demonstrate your feels to the team. I have seen people relate it to sports they play or family situations. Whatever is important to you and share with the team they will know that its genuine. When writing a story to help lead, think about how this came across.

LEARNING FROM ELDERS

Learning from mentors who have been in an organization longer is how you can grow from past experiences. We are always focused on new innovative ideas, but there are times when ideas have been tried in the past and have yet to work. Learning about what has occurred in the past is how you can improve. We don't want our organization to be stuck on a hamster wheel. Running in circles and never getting anywhere. This is no way to build a career.

Lessons learned from the past can set us on a path to improve and make it better. We have to understand that if we keep doing things the same way over and over, we aren't going to change or improve. With any team, you will be stuck if you don't have the opportunity to change. Think about the organizations that don't change. What happens to them when they fade away from memory?

There used to be a company called Blockbuster (a retailer that rented DVDs to customers before streaming existed), but they were too slow to evolve. They kept doing things the same, and the company has now vanished.

Another example is Toys R'Us, who partnered with Amazon as their exclusive toy distributor. Amazon didn't follow through on the deal and let others sell toys on their platform. By the time Toys R'Us got out of the agreement, they had missed the opportunity to develop their own e-commerce website.

We are creatures of habit and would like everything to stay the same, but things rarely ever do; we see change occurring rapidly. Now, we must work to embrace what we learned to be better prepared for our future.

This is vital in teams; the best leaders are the ones that learn along the way. The learning brings better results that help all team members achieve.

OPEN TO TEAM IDEAS

Openness to ideas and clear communication are the essence of outstanding leadership. Teams that communicate often feel more connected to each other and share ideas across the business.

We have gotten to a point where people are discouraged from sharing or having disagreements. Keeping everything in doesn't encourage a positive environment where teams can learn. Open communication within areas are built on trust that we learned in the elephant's lessons.

Organizations that blame each other and don't have that trusting environment, try to be open before they are ready, which causes the business to suffer. Staff across the organization have negative feelings, which can run any business into the ground faster than any profits could be achieved.

People are strange when they don't know something. They develop their own thoughts and create rumors based on those thoughts. Rumors lead to misinterpretation of facts and understandings of what is happening in a business. Large organizations think keeping things quiet is the best way to achieve results. This makes the rumor mill the best way for most organization members to find information. It's only sometimes correct information, but it's highly effective in finding out what may be occurring at the higher levels in a business. The rumor mill is, unfortunately, sometimes the heart of the company if large organizations don't communicate the truth. The best way to squash this would be to share more information in multiple mediums so that people can always fact-check anything happening on the rumor mill.

Feeling connected is an essential aspect of a team's success. To achieve this, you need to have consistent and clear communication. Some organizations use email, social media, and town hall meetings to ensure the correct information is offered to all within the company. All of these methods have positives and negatives. The best way to stay on the positive side of communication is to ensure your focused communication is accurate and succinct. When too much information is shared simultaneously, some people will comprehend all the details, while others will skim. The best way to ensure teams are connected is for leaders to interpret the company-wide information into specific bullets and then share this. When speaking to colleagues who are team leaders and management, employees consider this a highly effective method.

THE ZEBRA'S SUMMARY

The Zebra lessons taught us that teams are made up of many different people that have different qualities that bring a group together and succeed. The simple solution in their mind is storytelling, respecting each other and talking is the answer for teams to build cohesion. It may be that simple.

We can change our team by using these ideas:

- Teach processes through storytelling and allow elders to mentor new team members so both feel empowered.
- Each person is an individual; find a way for each team member to so they can help meet the team's goals.
- Share as much information as you can with the team, from what is happening at meetings you

attend and thoughts that you have on the team's directions. Listen to the feedback your team has great ideas that will help everyone grow.

As professionals, managers, and leaders, we should consider providing an environment that includes these ideas to encourage teamwork.

MEERKATS - MEETING

Katie learned in the story that meetings and communication are essential for team leaders to ensure we can keep our projects meeting objectives.

LEADER LED MEETINGS:

Leader-led meetings are what you expect to be a regular meeting. This is where a supervisor is talking to a group in a meeting. This can be done in person or via Zoom. I have always found that these meetings work better with an agenda. An agenda (I attached an example at the end of this section) is the best way to give everyone at the meeting the topics that will be discussed and how they can contribute to the meeting.

- A classic style of this meeting is for the team leader to sit at the head of the table and then ask each person around the room for an update on what they have accomplished since they last met. After everyone around the room spoke, the leader would talk about any updates to the organization. This style is not team focused. It meets all the criteria for a meeting, but sometimes, people zone out when they are not interested in what other team members are sharing.

- A second style is for the leader to mention project deadlines and then ask each member to share how their areas are progressing. Each team member is asked to share who else they are working with to complete their part of the project. This additional person would then be asked to share with the initial person. By sharing the tasks and updates, they can provide a more detailed picture of the project status to the leader. This style is better than the classic style for team management since you are focused on the objective. Most people are engaged since missing an update could affect other project parts.

- A third style is for the leader to appoint someone else as the facilitator of the meeting. This person would start a discussion topic that has come up in the team since the last met. The objective is to engage the group in open communication without the leader being present. The leader only talks if they need to add additional information. This is focused on how to have this facilitator lead the meeting to find out how about the project. This is a mentoring opportunity for the leader. It also allows all the team members to openly communicate without being directed. This last method is completely team-focused and helps build trust by enabling others to oversee the meeting.

All of the leader-led meetings are used in a department of a company. They are predictable to the employees, so they are designed to be non-threatening since they know what to expect each time. The predictability is good, but it can still leave some topics not discussed. Which is problematic, but any of these methods demonstrates to employees that the leader cares. Leaders could be better, but each attempt allows employees to feel that their impact matters to the company.

———

TIP: A short discussion on a topic for ten minutes can be very effective in covering high-level points. If a meeting topic continues for twenty minutes, stop the conversation. Schedule a separate meeting to discuss the matter to give it the attention it deserves.

BRAINSTORMING MEETINGS

These meetings are specifically geared toward developing ideas for the team. It is assumed that the team already knows the objective but needs to understand the variety of options necessary to complete the project.

Brainstorming meetings are one of my favorite types of meetings. A brainstorming meeting is focused on developing multiple ideas on how to solve the problem. Generating ideas is focused on the leader facilitating the discussion and asking opening questions that make the team think about the situation. Each group would work individually to develop a minimum of six solutions. These can be anything from building a solution with technology to working with outside vendors or with some wild guesses. That is why sometimes wild ideas help people generate other alternatives that should always be considered. No matter what the ideas are, the more you can generate, the more it will allow the larger group to figure out which is feasible.

I remember my boss asked me for the WAG of a project cost. This was my Wild Ass Guess because he needed a general idea of cost. It would be a partial analysis, but it gave us a starting point. From that point, we could brainstorm the various parts to see the actual costs.

An Example: We decided to implement a new Wi-Fi system at our university. We were focused on offering the best experience since we were experiencing trouble with the current vendor. We scheduled the meeting with a few teams: the technology, the implementation, the client, and the management teams. Each team member present was given a post-it notepad and then instructed to write down at least three answers per question, no speaking or using technology. Write down one reply per Post-It note, but more than three possible answers are desired per question. After each question, we gave the teams 45-60 seconds to write down their answers. Sometimes, questions arise in this section, so I pause before asking my first question since it may take a minute for everyone to grasp the concept if they haven't done one of these sessions. (Explanations would happen later in these sessions; quick answers are the best.)

1. We then started brainstorming sessions by asking each team member to answer this question:
2. What experience did we want the client to encounter with the system?
3. What is their biggest worry about this implementation?
4. What the best timeline is for implementation?
5. What do you think will be a successful implementation?

After everyone wrote all this down, we collected them, posted them on the whiteboard, and began to address each item in a more collaborative discussion.

We go around the room and ask each person to explain their ideas.

1. No idea is discounted, and the team will review every suggestion.
2. Each team member discusses their points, and the team decides if it is worth considering by adding a star to the post.

3. After each idea is discussed, the team needs to eliminate the ideas that aren't feasible.
4. The objective is to narrow it down to maximum three ideas or less.

The leader then works to come up with a short description for each proposal that is going forward. The team would produce a one or two page document to share with senior leadership. A recommendation of which ideas the team thinks are more reasonable. Senior leadership can use this as their guide to making a final decision.

A brainstorming meeting can be a team-building moment. This is a shared experience opportunity for your team to work together, collaborate, and hear concerns from all different sides.

When you implement this type of meeting, you break down everybody's anxiety and help them overcome their concerns. Team members in attendance will understand the goal and may be on different pages when they start any of these brainstorming meetings. After the conclusion of the meeting, attendees understand where other points of view are coming from. Teams that have done this are more prepared to deal with surprise situations than ones that haven't.

STAND-UP MEETING

A stand-up meeting is a 10-minute or less meeting. Retail organizations have this in the morning, with the team standing in a
circle. The session begins with a leader updating the team on
what's to be accomplished for the day. It's focused, specific, and
brief. The sharing of information builds trust with the team.
They can ask a couple of questions.

Tell your team what's happening and your expectations. Clearly
explain what will occur during that day. This ensures that
everyone is on the same page.

Many organizations utilize stand-up meetings such as retail,
technology teams, and sports. The leader wants to give a quick
update to focus the effort of everyone on the task at hand.
Sometimes, this is used as a motivation opportunity, but it's
always brief and focused.

If you plan on running one of these stand-up meetings, ensure
you have summed up all the information to share quickly.
Don't hold back information that may be important. People
can recognize that quickly. This is a day when the more you can
share will help everyone know that you are empowering them to
be there for the customers. Leaders must give up authority so
everyone can implement the objective. Stand-up meetings are
the way to do this. Leaders always need to remember the team
comes first. By demonstrating this daily, they will always be
there with you in the good and challenging times.

Agenda:

In any meeting, an Agenda is vitally important. The agenda is a straightforward document with the name, date/time and location at the top. It contains a list of bulleted topics to discuss. Enclosed is a sample agenda:

Agenda for Today's (NAME OF MEETING) Meeting - Date

LOCATION OF THE MEETING

1. Discussion topic on changing our marketing strategy for a Pitch competition

2. Awards

3. Recognition of Team Members

- Kelly
- Roger

4. Plans for the next event.

- Meeting with Outside Partners
- Meeting with Internal Partners
- Follow-up discussion on strategy moving forward

5. Budget

6. Next Meeting date?

THE ANTS - THREE OBJECTIVES

The Ants taught us three Key Objectives that leaders need to embrace. Here are brief summaries of each:

EMPOWERMENT:

Leaders who excel learn to empower their teams with information. They share what they know, then let employees ask questions to dive into the topics with as many details as needed. As a young leader, I remember when my Vice President (VP) met with a list of top issues we would need to discuss. They included email issues, too much storage, and the transition to cloud solutions.

He would explain that we would be moving our central personnel system to our cloud provider. The team would ask questions on timelines, resources, and financial risks. These conversations were focused and productive. Then, he empowered us to devise a plan for each area.

This trust in us was his empowerment to each of our teams. He knew we would devise a collaborative plan and then allow us to execute it. He never asked about the details. He was focused on the high-level objective to get the project completed.

The empowerment he granted allowed us to feel dedicated and driven to meet his goals. Everyone had a feeling of ownership toward ensuring the VP met his goals. There was no backstabbing or not sharing details. Everyone cared about each other to ensure we kept on track.

Empowerment can ensure teams can efficiently work on their project and know that the VP has their back. They don't feel like they are being put out there without support. As a leader, when you can do this, you will get results you could never have imagined.

Empowerment - Focus on helping each person grow with their path. As a leader, you must provide technology, motivation, and guidance for people to succeed in their careers. If you can, they can conquer any objective in front of them.

Our goal is always to develop people, not only complete the work.

TRUST

Trust is our leadership ability to share the whole truth with your team. It's our openness to let them know a company's financial state, the status of projects, and the weak points inside of an organization. That will show our trust in them.

1. The first step in building trust is the sharing of information.
2. The second step is demonstrating as a leader, you can relate to what is occurring with your team members.
3. The third step in building trust is listening to my coworkers. Hearing about their families, successes at work, and failures allows me to see life through their eyes. Listening can provide you, as the leader, the guidance and direction that isn't said in everyday conversations.

These are the steps, but trust is knowing that you can rely on them. It only happens slowly, but it can be built. Leaders need to accept they are the ones who hold the ownership to build this two-way street between leader and staff. This requires us to have complete confidence in them and, in turn, they of us. This is what the key to trust is in the workplace.

Building trust is the key to a happy workplace because even on the worst days, the Trust you built with your team can overcome any obstacle.

COMMUNICATION

Communication is our ability to use verbal and non-verbal cues to share information. The Ants used it to ensure everyone knew what was happening in a colony. We can use it in our departments or areas to ensure our colleagues and staff have consistent information.

The ants had mastered the ability of communication, which is critical to integrating culture within the communication you utilize. I have seen that when we utilized our own internal acronyms and naming objects. This blended culture and communication in ways the team had their own language. This has helped the area strive beyond expectations because when things were occurring, we could identify the system, space, or project with a name that made sense to the whole organization. We used the word Greenhouse to represent a space for growing new ideas. This helped everyone to quickly know all about the space that was focused on that. Whenever a new service wanted to be implemented, if it didn't go along with the core mission of growing new ideas, that service was specifically ruled out.

We used other names for equipment specifically themed on Pokemon, Marvel, or Spongebob. These were themes that were easily identifiable by our teams. We used Wonder Woman and Hulk to represent different technological equipment. Whenever we mentioned these names, the whole team could tell you about it. This built a language that was unique to the teams, and they felt special since they could be included within a team that understood that communication has parallels to teamwork.

When communicating, are there ideas that can be communicated more effectively by using terms that represent you? I work with a colleague who runs a laptop loaner program; when they talk, they ask about where a specific laptop is, but they have three benches where work is done. They call them Bench 1, 2, and 3. It confuses people to the point where they don't know where things are being served. I would name these with specific places depending on the function of the bench.

Naming may seem simple but have you considered using it at home. I purchased a pool vacuum, an automatic robot that climbs the sides and bottom to clean out all the leaves and debris that fall into the water. We call it Gizmo, so whenever we need to clean it or take it out of the water. We use Gizmo, and everyone in my house knows what we are talking about quickly and efficiently.

The best communication you could offer your team is efficient, quick, and truthful conversations.

A term that we found that helped resonate when onboarding a new staff was ICC. It signified our philosophy with three simple words: Impression, Communication, and Collaboration (ICC).

Our focus is on giving our customers the correct impression of our services, effectively communicating with them about offering guidance to complete their tasks, and collaborating with them as they progress their projects.

When we did this and lived by this philosophy, the team communication effectively ensured the customer's needs were the cornerstone of our services. When you return to work, consider how to use these concepts in your workplace.

Choosing what to apply is different for each team. Things from the Ants may be more appropriate than the Meerkats. It doesn't matter which you choose to change, but taking the first step and making a change will lead you to great leadership. You will be taking your first step on the Wolf's Path.

QUOTE

Leadership is about making others better as a result of your
presence,
and
making sure that impact lasts in your absence

- Sheryl Sandberg

PART THREE
TEAM DEVELOPMENT &
ACTIVITIES

Team development is an unspoken area that is needed for us to succeed at work and in our personal lives. We sometimes don't feel team activities are essential, but they break down boundaries to allow us to learn about the real person. As a team leader, I have a collection of activities that are effective in getting teams to collaborate.

Enclosed are a few activities that I have found most successful. I didn't create all of these. Others developed them, and I modified them to meet my situation. I selected team activities that only needed limited resources. The resources needed for these can be found in an office supply cabinet. This made it easier for a leader to implement. If you want more ideas, please reach out to us at any time.

.   .   .

These team activities are best used at a meeting or a retreat. However, if you decide to use these, think about how the team would feel as a result of the activity. Ensuring you know what you want to gain will help the activity work better with your team. After you implement these please let us know what happened. Sharing results helps us to improve the activities., Please reach out to me through any of my contact details.

ACTIVITY 1: WHO ARE YOU? INTRODUCTIONS

The introduction activity is about taking a group of people 25 or less and having them learn about each other to see if any areas of similarities exist.

Resources: no resources are needed

Steps:

- Gather all your team into a circle.
- As the facilitator, you join the circle. You are the starting and ending point.
- Explanation to the group.
- We are all going to go around the circle from left to right.
- Please tell us your name, something you like to do, and one pet peeve you have in life.
- Each person to the left after their introduction will repeat each of what the previous team members said until they get back to the facilitator. This includes

their name, what the like and pet peeve for each team member. This may be two people if you're the third person or 12 if you are further along in the circle.

- As the facilitator, you will go first and last. At the end, you will have to introduce each person in the circle, say their name, like, and pet peeve.
- Always start with the person standing on your left and go clockwise.
- When the circle comes back to you, step out of the circle into the center and look at each person in the eye as you go from your right all the way back to the left.

Notes:

1. Most people get upset about this since they think they can't remember information about each person, but we always find others in the circle who will help each other.

1. Don't say anything; let the first five people figure it out with each other's help, but if by the 8th person they forget, you can encourage them to help each other.

1. In adults, usually by the 8th or 9th person, there becomes an understanding by the group on how hard it is to remember each person's information. There is cheering or clapping when people remember all the information.

1. Try not to have friends stand next to each other, it's better that they separate.

<u>After action debrief:</u>
(This is where you talk to your team about the activity that was completed)

- Did anyone find someone who had similar interests?
- Did anyone learn something that was new to them?
- What is the benefit of doing this activity?
- This activity opens everyone up to building a culture of sharing personal and not-so-personal details. The group will be able to find something about each other interesting. Then at your first meal break, we usually see people sitting together asking about their interests in this activity.

The session opens the team to learning everyone's name and having something to help them associate the name with an activity. This is a technique that psychologists have found in brain studies that the best way to remember someone's name is to have another key fact about them. The key fact, such as something they like or pet peeve in this case, gives people two ways to sort the information in their minds.

As you go through your exercise, please modify it as needed.

ACTIVITY 2: - HOT POTATO BRAINSTORMING

The hot potato exercise is a simple moving a small squish football around to keep the team moving while simultaneously brainstorming on how to solve an issue.

The activity is geared toward helping people communicate quickly and share ideas that may not come up in natural conversations.

Resources: squishy football or similar sports ball that is made of foam and is light. A timer or phone with a stopwatch.

Steps: Ask your team to break up into teams of 6 people maximum. At least four people are required for this activity. Have the people stand in a circle looking at each other.

- Hand one of them a ball, football, or similar. It must be small and can fit into someone's hand, and it must be gentle so that if someone catches it, they won't get hurt.

- Tell the teams your objective is to move the ball around the group in any fashion you like, but as you move it there are a few rules.
- Every person must touch the ball before it can be returned to starting person, which signifies the end of round 1.
- Teams will get 3-5 rounds, depending on your team's needs.
- When you pass the ball, you must share a thought to solving one of these problems.
- Your statement can't be more than five words
- Each team will be timed and asked for their solution at the end.
- The team with the best solution in the shortest time will receive a prize.

Notes:

The problems I used here for examples are ones we can use globally but if you have a specific company issue, you can replace it with that.

1. How do you solve climate change?
2. How do you enhance communication in your organization?
3. What is the way to end all starvation?
4. How do we live in space successfully?
5. How do we move people from Microsoft Word to Google Docs (assuming your organization uses Microsoft Word)?
6. How do you teach people to stay organized with their to-do list?
7. How do we solve the water crisis for the world?

Additional Notes:

- If you have multiple teams they should go simultaneously trying to find a solution for the same problems.

- Post the scores of the teams after each specific rounds on a whiteboard for the whole group to see.

- Generating some competition here will help them develop new ideas

After action debrief:
Individually discuss the solutions. Gain feedback from teams.

As a facilitator is it not your role to decide if any of the solutions are good or bad, your goal is to keep the conversation moving so these teams will start to see each other as colleagues. The connections these colleagues are making are the key.

This activity is to build a shared experience that will open the team members' thoughts, allowing them to see how everyone has value. Individuals work in different areas of a company, but they are all committed to delivering superb services. Understanding this will encourage individuals to work together across different areas.

ACTIVITY 3: THE BALL GAME

This aims to get the team to toss a ball. See the benefit of working together as a team ito develop quick thinking and communicating.

Resources: beach ball

Steps:

1. Each group forms a circle. Teams should be no more than 8 people
2. Each member has to pass the ball to another member in front of them.
3. You can not pass the ball to the person beside you (to the left or right). Either its passed to the person two away from you or across from you.
4. The person passing the ball must call out the name of the person they are throwing the ball too
5.]The ball should not fall to the floor. When passing the ball only the receiver of the ball may touch it.

6. *The ball should be thrown gently across to the person.*
7. Each person only has 3 seconds to hold and then pass the ball.

1. If the ball falls to the ground, the thrower of the ball says the persons wrong name, or you hold the ball too long. You must restart with the first person again.

1. Once each team member has touched the ball the team has completed the game.

The Second Round this is a timed event:
The group times itself.
Then the times are announced in the room

Third Round is a timed event and the top two teams get a prize.
The timer will start when the facilitator yells go!

After Action Debrief:

1. What did you do that made you more successful? What didn't work?
2. How do these ideas from this activity relate to your work?
3. What would you do differently as a result of this activity in the future with teams?

The overall goal of this activity is to have the group focus on knowing the people on the team and working together to ensure they pass the ball all around the group in a way that isn't clockwise or counterclockwise.

ACTIVITY 4: BUILDING OUR SKYSCRAPER.

The team must build a free-standing skyscraper to hold up a ping pong ball with the supplies given. This activity focuses on allowing a team to communicate, learn how to use limited resources, and creatively think through a problem quickly.

Resources: 30 large popsicle sticks, one piece of paper (8 ½ x 11 inches), two rubber bands and 10 small popsicle sticks. Ping Pong balls

Steps: Each team will have 6 minutes to build a free-standing skyscraper with the supplies provided.

- You can't break the popsicle sticks
- The paper can be rippled in half, if needed but not required
- Build this structure so that at the end of the time, it can hold a ping-pong ball

- The structure has to stand on its own without anyone propping it up. It also can't lean on any wall or desk in the room.
- Lay out the supplies and once the teams are at the table. Have the begin.

After Action Debrief:

1. What was the most challenging part of this activity?
2. How did the team communicate to meet the goal?
3. What creative solutions did you develop during the activity?

The concept here is to have the team work together to think creatively about making a skyscraper. The supplies given are less than most people would use. Some groups would use all the supplies, but most forget that the two rubber bands can be used to hold different sticks together. They forget the rubber bands exist.

This is a difficult task given the supplies and time limit, but understanding how teams deal with stress is important since in all our jobs, stress comes up. When you are able to see this before it occurs, you can work to implement solutions that help teams work through this.

Leaders use these techniques to gain an understanding of areas that they need to improve. This exercise teaches individuals on how to deal with difficult situations and know there is always a solution.

ACTIVITY 5: KITCHEN BUILD COMPETITION

The Kitchen Build activity focuses on having teams work together for a shared experience. In this activity, teams of 3 or 4 must work together with the supplies provided to build anything available in the kitchen. This activity focuses on having teams utilize limited supplies to prototype the idea.

Resources: A few cardboard boxes, scissors, tape, paper clips, pens, and rubber bands. Popsicle sticks and pipe cleaners if you have them, colored markers and crayons. Upbeat music to play during the activity.

Steps: This can be done in a group of up to 30 people.

1. Set up the supplies at tables before the activity starts.
2. Remove all the chairs (if you can have people stand its better; you can add back chairs for people that have a disability)

3. Break apart the group in to teams of three or four people.
4. Assign a specific table, for each group
5. Explain to the groups that you will have 8-10 minutes (modify as you see fit), to build something that will help you in the kitchen. Brainstorm as a group to develop an idea and use the supplies necessary to design something. This should be a working prototype. The design and how life like it is will help the judge decide the winner.
6. Start the timer and play some music (make the music loud so it's difficult to hear)
7. Walk around the room to see if there are any questions.
8. Groups can build tables, chairs, utensils, pots, pans, almost anything
9. At two minutes, announce the time left. (lower the music slightly)
10. At one minute, announce the time left
11. When time is up, please stop the music and have everyone stop working.
12. Walk around the room have each team explain their idea and select the winner based on the one that is most functional and looks most like the life like.
13. Groups should be able to describe their reason for creating this and how it will benefit them in the kitchen.

Notes:

- The winner will gain bragging rights, and the team will be given a certificate of winning the Kitchen challenge.

<u>After action debriefs:</u>

1. What did you learn about your teammate's work style?
2. Would you communicate differently knowing how others work?
3. What was something that your team did extremely well?
4. What did your team need to work on to complete the task?

This activity is focused on having teams work together in an experience where they can do something that may be easy or difficult, but by working together, you will be able to see how others approach a problem. Each approach may be different but knowing how others work will be helpful in the future. You will be able to ensure when you have them on the team you can collaborate since you know their style. It also builds a sense of comradery since you all have experienced the same task on the same day.

This activity is pure fun and work can be fun.

ACTIVITY 6 – MAGIC CREDIT CARD

The Magic Credit card is focused on giving everyone an unlimited credit card, we are curious to see how people will utilize this card. Anything spent on this magic credit card must be used for someone else. This opens up your team to talk about things they care about rather than themselves. This activity is focused on communication and evaluating how you can focus on others in your life. When you work on a team, it's important to focus on the other team members rather than yourself.

Resources: A piece of paper with the attached questions and pens

Steps: Best done in a group of 10 or less performed at the start of a meeting.

1. Ask each person to complete the Magic Credit card sheet (available at the end of this activity)
2. For the Who, please list the name of the person

3. For the What, please list the item that you would purchase for them.
4. For the Why, please list the reason you are purchasing this.
5. Give them 4 minutes maximum to complete the sheet
6. Ask each person to share one of their choices with the group.

After Action debrief:

This activity is focused on people; we spend so much time with colleagues that we forget that they have lives, families, and interests outside of work. This activity allows people to think about others. It's the beginning of opening the team to acknowledge each other in a new, deeper way. I found this activity to build deeper connections.

Ask the group questions to see how they felt about this activity.

1. How difficult was it to choose a person?
2. What emotions did you experience while thinking through this?
3. Did you find this activity to make you think more about others?
4. Is there something that you would want the team to know that is a follow-up to this activity? (Maybe you are dealing with something outside of work that may affect work)

The connections and communications of this activity may start slowly but have helped teams overcome boundaries normally built when the work takes precedence.

<u>The Magic Credit Card Sheet:</u>

The Magic Credit Card ... A card that you never have to Pay Back.

You could purchase any one item for three different people in your life, and this card you would never have to pay it back. What would you purchase? Remember its magic

1. Person 1:
2. Who:
3. What:
4. Why:
5. Person 2:
6. Who:
7. What:
8. Why;
9. Person 3:
10. Who:
11. What:
12. Why:

Reach out to us for a formatted sheet.

ADDITIONAL RESOURCES

The author developed additional resources and advice where you can learn more information. Please follow us on social media and join our newsletter

Instagram: @theinnovativepath
YouTube: @icreateXP
LinkedIn: linkedin.com/company/icreate-experiences/

To join the newsletter and find the associated support materials, visit us at
www.icreatexp.com

Please feel free to reach out to us at
info@icreatexp.com

ABOUT THE AUTHOR

David Ecker is a Stony Brook University alumnus who has worked at the university for 27+ years in technology management and leadership roles. In addition, he is an entrepreneur who founded many businesses and is currently focused on Wolf Steps, a company that is working to help others advance their careers and life aspirations. This is David's second book in this series.

He focuses on leadership skills, innovation, the entrepreneurial practices, and technology. He believes hands-on learning is the future for success. David founded WolfieTank, a pitch competition for young entrepreneurs to present their ideas to a panel of Stony Brook alumni. As well as SUNY LI Pitch Fest a pitch competition between Long Island SUNY business schools.

David made it possible for Stony Brook University to respond to the shortage of PPE during COVID by creating five thousand 3D-printed face shields with a team from the Long Island community for first responders. He presented at TedX Stony Brook in 2013. His talk "When life throws you a curve ball" demonstrates how teachers can learn from students.

David holds an MBA Graduate Certificate in Innovation and Entrepreneurship from Empire State University, a Master of

Science in Technological Systems Management from Stony Brook University, and a Bachelor of Science from Stony Brook University.

David lives on Long Island with his family.

instagram.com/theinnovativepath

linkedin.com/in/david-ecker-5a62902

tiktok.com/@icreatexp

5 Lessons for Success - Wolf Path Book

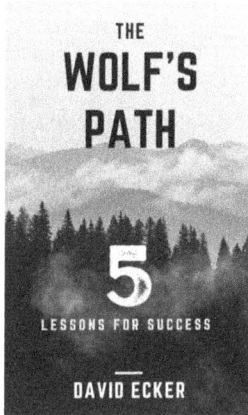

Success is within your reach.

Find five of the lessons that we need to turn a quiet existence into a successful and purpose-driven life in this complex world. Joe was gliding through life without purpose and didn't have the skills to survive and thrive. When a change was thrust upon him he needed to quickly learn to stand on his own.

Joe, Katie, and Summer's story demonstrates how we can overcome any challenge if we have the tools necessary for success and are willing to do the hard work. The answers are right in front of us if we just open our eyes and follow the path.

This easy-to-read story teaches us that when we reach a bend in the road or when we think we've hit a dead end, we can open ourselves to wonderful and fulfilling changes that we never expected.

$1200 and a Dream - An Entrepreneurs's Guide

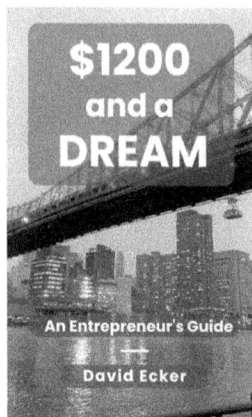

A practical guide for entrepreneurs, we help you move from running in circles to grabbing hold of your dreams by focusing on your goals and utilizing your skills and passion. We put each topic into a section broken down into individual subjects, real-life examples, and questions that make you think. Learning is a process; this is your guide to move you in the right direction for starting the business.

Our focus is an approach that includes hands-on learning to present topics and give you exercises to look within yourself for the answers. Specific skills such as Networking, Risk, Presentation, and Failure transcend careers to move us toward engagement. To do this, we focus on understanding the entrepreneurs' strengths and work ethic to determine our inner strengths in these fields.

www.ingramcontent.com/pod-product-compliance
Lightning Source LLC
Chambersburg PA
CBHW060759050426
42449CB00008B/1457